Italian Sketches

Garrett Rittenberg

Bowery Books
New York

Copyright © 2020 Garrett Rittenberg
Bowery Books, New York

Italian Sketches

ISBN For this edition: 978-1-7344202-4-1

Book formatting by: **Last Mile Publishing**

First Edition Published: July 1st, 2020

For Craig Rittenberg

May we be young and in Rome again

Introduction

This is a diary. A daily record of what I sought and experienced during the four months I spent wandering around Italy some years ago. After rereading this diary, I realized that Italy is always a good subject no matter how it is approached. Everyone's take carries some weight. Each word in a book of travel is an attempt to retain something of the past, and a diary is a useful tool for retention. This is by no means a thesis or a final word on Italy, Italians or Italian culture, as I do not seek any grand conclusions about Italy nor did I wish to pontificate too deeply upon Italian culture, the world is familiar with its greatness. I wanted to have my time there, because time in Italy is significant. It is a brief view into its culture. More succinctly it is my view.

I wanted to know Italy, and by diligently taking notes almost every evening while traveling around the country, I was able to gain a clear picture of the journey I had taken and the things I witnessed. Writing down one's travels gives the pleasure of traveling twice. Perhaps it is a way of simply making a journey easily remembered, but I believe it indeed brings one closer to the country itself. I had spent no more than ten days in Italy in my entire life when I decided to spend a whole winter traveling across the country. This short amount of time continually bothered me and caused a deep dissatisfaction with my previously blurry eyed young self who turned out to be a terrible witness to a place that deserves nothing but wide-eyed attention and admiration. So, as I went elsewhere and for one reason or another did not make my way to Italy, my desire and curiosity steadily grew. Italy was becoming more important to me. It was not just something on a list of things to do, but rather an experience to be had that could possibly shape my perspective and character in a new and pleasurable manner. The more I thought about it the more my respect grew for the country. I took it seriously, as is my wont when encountering anything as grand and historic as Italy.

I would regularly hear about Italy from all walks of life— from the cruise ship tourist to the mountaineering adventurer to the person who every year only vacations in Italy, and even the person who had only been to one country other than their own— Italy. I must, indeed, confess one reason I did not visit Italy. My failure to visit Italy was, in fact, not entirely a failure to act, but rather a purposeful avoidance of the country— an avoidance grown out of a desire to not merely spend a few days in one Italian city or another, which seemed to me like a frivolous endeavor. At times I thought of it as an insult to such a grand place. It only seemed proper to at least try to spend an extended amount of time in Italy, to get acquainted properly with it, to understand it as best as one could. I wanted a 'Grand Tour' of the country, not a tour. W.H. Auden rightly described Italy as a poem, and I had a terrible desire to memorize, like a poem, as many Italian scenes as I could, for I felt it could only enrich my mind. And this could only be done by making the journey last for a few months.

I did not seek to settle in one city or village. I wanted to see all that I could and by regularly moving around I gained a sense of the regional differences of the country, much like the differences any country might possess. The urban to the rural, the poor to the well off, differences in speech, cuisine, religious practice, and work were made clear and more recognizable simply by observing them as I moved about the country. Sometimes people would unabashedly let you know how they felt about another region of the country. At a barbershop in Milan, the barber cutting my hair constantly joked with me about the way one of his fellow barbers, a Neapolitan, spoke. And at one point said with some seriousness that, "he does not speak Italian he speaks, 'animale.'" On the trains in southern Italy, the loudspeakers shout out the usual instructions to mind the gaps and which station was next, but they also warned passengers that it is a crime to not comply with a request for documents as well as the illegality of striking a member of the train staff. It was resoundingly different in the north where no such thing was mentioned on any of the loudspeakers.

When one has looked at Italy for a long time they are bound to look at the rest of the world in a different manner— if you observe so much beauty you become better at observing both beauty and its opposites— you understand it all so much better, because Italy is a visual teacher— a masterful one at that. After returning home from four months in Italy, I was a different person. My mind was made clear, I had much to say, and my thought process and speaking had improved. I was garrulous, not just to speak of Italy, but just to speak. I had developed a concise and alert sense of taste and distaste. A few months spent in Italy is as good as any education, perhaps better than most, and certainly more enjoyable than any classroom or book could ever be.

Italy has the ability to make you very rich. To soak your mind in culture and beauty, in the history and collective grace of Italians. Italy allows for one's sense of sight to go past its perceived limits and abilities.

Never did I think my eyes could reach such a heightened state of pleasure. Italy made me realize that I had been taking my eyes for granted. It is funny to say, but upon returning I felt as though my eyes had been bathing in some sort of aesthetic cultural marinade. My eyes never experienced so much beauty for such an extended period of time. This can become a kind of addiction, but it is not the kind of addiction that leaves one crashing down when not receiving another dose of scenery or culture, unable to ever reach a previously heightened state, it somehow enhances the next experience, whatever it may be, each and every time. I must admit, all those days in Italy was drug-like, because so many times did I think of the word intoxication. But there was no overdosing on art, architecture, beautiful landscapes or delicious food. It was all good.

Italy is obviously an old place, but it is a modern crossroads, indeed one of the largest and most significant in the world. There is hardly a city or village, a beach or a mountain in Italy that has gone unvisited by travelers from dozens of countries. All of Italy is known and has been found before. It is not a place of unique discovery, but rather a place to explore and make something of or take something from its treasurable culture. And like all cultures different from one's own, it can be a kind of mirror to show us what we are not— perhaps what we wish we could be.

Italy is like a portrait, it is also full of some of the most beautiful portraits that exist, and from Italy some of the most beautiful portraits are created and then flung out to other parts of the earth. It is a well of artistic endeavor and inspiration. Italy succeeds in being a generous canvas for the world, because upon visiting Italy it is almost inevitable to encounter in the galleries, museums, on street corners or even cliff edges— young people from around the world who have descended upon Italy with a creative urge to become artists for a few moments or years— some devoted to art for a lifetime, others having a brief flirtation, in order to sketch the paintings, sculptures and architectural doings of Italians. They know that by depicting the artistic and natural fruits of Italy they will gain a piece of it and they will become something more, perhaps it will even make them whole if need be. They are mostly done through drawings and charcoal sketches, and there are even young plein air painters putting themselves on display.

Time is something made very clear to you in Italy and I quickly realized that four months is not a very long time in the history of Italy. That is why recording what I saw was important to me, for if it were not a record of a lifetime of experiences in Italy, it was at least my experiences. I chose not to draw, sketch or simply reconfigure the beautiful scenes I came across with a brush or piece of charcoal, but rather I hoped to do that through words. After going from one end of Italy to the other the country is now a portrait complete in my mind. Perhaps the small corners of Puglia and Liguria are absent, but some paintings are still beautiful when there is a space or two left blank. It is a difficult endeavor to create a perfect portrait of Italy and perhaps that should be left to the masters of every medium or simply just to Italians themselves, but everyone is somewhat entitled to create their own sketches of Italy. These are mine.

Diary

December 6th   Rome

The prime minister resigned today, but nobody cares. Why should I? I did not make any attempt to find out why as it did not seem to matter. A cool gray morning, slightly wet, it feels like Rome is by the sea. The yelping barks of toy dogs resemble squawking seagulls and are preferable to hollering crowds. It is not tourist madness in the city at the moment. It is again an Italian city for the time being, medieval and conservative.

I am sad to be alone in this beautiful place, though I suspect its beauty will change my disposition at some point. I decided to wander by myself, and not pay much attention to my direction, so long as it was in Italy. Traveling alone is much easier for the most part. Friendships get tested during travel, and I have no desire to be testing anything at the moment. A friendship is much like holding on to a pigeon which is more or less like trying to catch one. It always appears my fault when it ends. I am never satisfied in them, and the people I want to be close with are the elusive types. The interesting ones are always that way. Company, so much of it, is about passing time, saying less, mentally communicating or just being present. I believe my discontent has something to do with my awareness of freedom. I fear a trap. I fear boredom. I fear the inability to move. I suppose that means there is little contentment in me, and naturally my eye looks at other places. That is not a good formula for happiness.

At the San Luigi di Francesco I asked the man selling postcards to point me towards the Caravaggio and he said it was in the last chapter. It is reassuring to see the incompletely blended brush marks amongst some of Caravaggio's paintings. I wanted to see *The Calling of St. Matthew* from even closer. The light coming in from the window gave the same sensation of reading ten novels. One of these images is worth a thousand images or a hundred thousand words. Its beaming light captures not just a present moment, but the before and after. It is more than just an image. It is a complete story. What else can one ask of a painting? It is the flash before one's last breath, every penultimate sense aroused. The canvas is left in the dark, and the light only comes on when someone puts some coins in the coin machine on the wall beside it. Like paying for a carnival ride.

There were some lesser Caravaggio paintings at Galleria Doria but still they were Caravaggio, they were all a pleasant sight to my eyes, but one cannot help but compare. I took a stroll through the Borghese Gardens and thought nothing but of how pleasant it is to be in Rome.

December 7th   Rome

Twelve years ago I was in the Vatican and today it appeared much smaller. The Sistine Chapel was brighter and clearer. It should not be a surprise, but often is, that so many devout flock to such places. Perhaps it is more for the art these days. Either way, it is the 'small people' who build these enormous institutions. Art everywhere is gaining traction as a cultural obsession or a kind of religion. It has its appeal, but like most everything that starts to lean towards a cultish disposition, it is better off done in private.

Sitting beside the Piazza del Popolo, two Mormon missionaries asked if I would like to watch a video on their iPad. It was two minutes of people hugging and so on, nothing was said, and at the end "Mormon.org," appeared on the screen. It was similar to a commercial for an erectile dysfunction pill.

There is always a desire to challenge these types, because of how devoutly they speak of God and Jesus Christ, divine callings and such. But I was in no mood to argue with these two girls, Taylor and Leigh. They were pleasant and asked more about me than they did to push their message. I mostly wondered why they saw me and thought I looked a good candidate for conversion. I cannot remember entirely, but they said something about a light upon me.

I asked how they got so lucky to be sent to Italy, and they said it was where the leader of the church said

5

they should go because that's what God told him. What luck. "Something told me to come here, too." I responded.

We thanked each other for the polite conversation and openness, and I remained, while they walked across the piazza to continue to work in the service of God and the great state of Utah.

I thought I was not having much fun and I was missing out on something by sitting there; people watching. But listening to them and watching them from a distance I no longer felt I was wasting my time and solitude. They were pleasant but also uneventful, and simple in such a way that inspired intense boredom. The repetitiveness of phrases and a constant subject of the church and God made the two of them appear as one person with an unfurnished mind, and me I felt by myself— in a room of conversation and thought. Back in my room I continued reading, Richard Ellman's, *James Joyce*, which felt more like divine inspiration than Mormon.org. Joyce is some kind of a Saint, an artistic Saint. We make our Saints and we choose them, too. Tonight, I chose Saint Joyce.

December 10th   Rome

I am older than everyone, I have come to realize.

Two old Italian ladies did their best to cut me in line at a pizza shop and gave up when I forcefully cut them back. How small we will always be— even amongst all this civilization. Perhaps civilization succeeds only in magnifying our primitive instincts. Elders resemble children sometimes, and often need to be reigned in.

I strolled with my zucchini pizza and stumbled into a tiny place dishing out large wooden boards covered in every conceivable cured meat and cheese and olive paste. There was even horse meat on offer. A blonde woman rapidly took orders, glasses broke on the floor and the Indian man slicing the meats carried out the three-foot-long boards covered with beautifully displayed meat to the tables. The food surrounds you like a perfectly manicured garden. It almost fills me with guilt to not go into each place I see with food so beautifully presented.

The stroll continued towards Sant Eustachio for espresso, but the little shop was plugged tight with people trying to get in and out. I sat across the street eating a cannolo and slowly went through the Times Literary Supplement. It has been a while since I read it and has been even longer since it had this many essays worth reading. A new book of Dutch stories including one by the architect Rem Koolhaas' father. Another book with a warts and all description of Scandinavians. I think it is enough with saying how great Scandinavia is, nobody wants to go there for the rest of their life, do they?

Tonight, at the espresso bar on the edge of Piazza del Popolo, the large waiter with a sad face made coffee and cleaned the counter. Every moment he stood still was meant for a melancholic portrait to be painted. His eyebrows were so bushy they looked as though they were to be paired with a luxurious fur coat of a similar hue. His apron straps were tight and humorously tied around his fat middle. The pants pulled up almost to the middle of the back. The clothes were worn, and small rips showed on the back of his pants. The bar he stood behind was pretty, but he was miserable, all the more because of how big he was. I wondered where his home was and hoped he was not unhappy there, too.

December 11th   Naples

It was the most interesting sky above the Piazza del Plebiscito. A deep gray with glowing pockets of light. The curvaceous trees on the edge of the piazza stood like illustrations. Italy swiftly intoxicates you so that everything appears as art. The whole world is on via Toledo and as Stendhal says, it is, "the most populous and cheerful street in the world."

I quickly found myself in a thick line of rambunctious people eagerly waiting to get fried pizza from Zia Esterino Sorbillo. At the bottom of via Toledo every pizza shop and café was stuffed full of people as if it were their first time here as it was for me. But this was just another day for the crowd of Neapolitans. The streets were flowing with families, shoppers moving in every direction, loudly with their garrulous voices. The voices make the air as crowded as the street. One lady excusing her way passed me for some napkins, spoke out loud the whole time, but to no one in particular.

People are dressed up like it is much colder than it is. It must be cold for them, I thought. I was drawn into the line of customers after looking at the Stuffoli in the window of Pintauro, the original Sfogliatella shop. Sfogliatella supposedly originates in Amalfi. For some reason, it reminded me of a place I have never been, but have often thought of visiting, Gaziantep, Turkey, which is supposed to have the best Baklava in the world. But it is much too dangerous to visit at the moment being so close to Syria. Pastry begets pastry, perhaps.

I have finished reading Ellman's biography of Joyce and bought a copy of Ulysses. I hope to do my best to read it in a reasonable amount of time. Ellman often quoted Finnegan's Wake to introduce a chapter and it is that book I find myself thinking about with regards to Joyce even more so than Ulysses. People always say weird or derisive things about it. Joyce's wife even said something like, why don't you write a normal book for people to read.

Ulysses takes place in one day and Finnegan's Wake in one night. An element of brevity is always preferable in a work of art, and perhaps quite necessary given the great lengths of each book. And since he is always talked of as a genius, I think it quite right that he would play with language and stretch it as far as he could with something like Finnegan's Wake. People as smart as Joyce tend to get bored and find more satisfaction with being a kind of provocateur. Provocation becomes their medium.

As far as his life, the main thing I always think of is his perpetual exile from Ireland. That was his identity. And being an eccentric Irishman and a Dubliner only succeeded in making him even more of an exile.

The life of an exile is appealing. It really is a non-committal life, a sort of promiscuity with where you live. An exile can never truly be a part of their place of exile. Some cultures are impervious. The good thing is that the place can never grab hold of you and turn you into your neighbor. Language and culture are constantly challenging you or rather confront you with your differentness. The self-exiled person wants freedom, and needs a little patience or just a desire to not go home.

I sat for dinner at a tiny place in Centro. Delicious food was served by an oddly mannered waiter. He had an unsettling way of using English that was jolting to your sense of security and naturally brings forth suspicion. He was constantly using the word 'buddy.' It was also the one English word he pronounced perfectly. I have come across this kind of 'tourist-English' before and it is often the sound of hustlers trying to rip you off. But this waiter was not ripping anyone off, he just sounded like he was.

He would also say things like 'don't be afraid, come in,' in a very slow tone, 'OK, buddy,' 'Everything all right, buddy?' 'Do you want some fresh pepper, buddy?' 'Are you ready for something to eat, buddy?' There was a deepness in his voice when he spoke English, and his staring eyes never blinked. When it was evident his creepiness was merely an aspect of his character and not a sign of things to come, I started to find his mannerisms and actions comical. Especially when he decided to put on a thick winter coat because he was cold and continued to serve tables.

December 12th   Naples

I took some notes for some time while sitting amongst the red velvet seats of the empty theater inside the Palazzo Reale. After finding out there were no Caravaggio paintings there, I got a ride up to Capodimonte to see the one there. It sits nicely at the end of a hallway about fifty yards long, perhaps more, come to think of it. It is noticeable from the furthest point. Two nice Brueghel paintings were there, too. As

I finished admiring the two paintings, I noticed the nice Dutch couple that sat next to me at dinner last night. They were particularly interested in the Brueghel's, which seemed fitting.

For some reason whenever I am far from home I have this constant desire to avoid being in cars or buses. I always want to walk. And thus, I walked all the way back down to Piazza del Plebiscito from Capodimonte. About two miles I think. There is a never-ending sound of scooters and the sight of laundry hanging from most every window. Some streets are so narrow the balconies are only a few feet from each other.

In the Centro and Quartieri Spagnoli everyone lives close together. It is loud and crowded. Something about it reminded me of Havana. Neapolitans and Cubans seem like cousins. Tonight, I turned down the wrong street in Quartieri Spagnoli. I walked further and further up the hill just wandering and hoping to find an even more local restaurant than the others I had already visited. As soon as I turned onto Vico Canale a Taverna Penta there was the sound of "psst, psst - hashish, hashish." I walked another twenty feet and there were some young kids playing soccer. Whoever did not have the ball seemed to be shouting. Another guy quickly walked towards me making himself noticed but never looked me in the eye just in my direction and shook his head as to say do not go down the street. I turned around casually, walked the other way and turned the corner down the hill. He followed me for about a block trying to get my attention to either sell me drugs or hope I would do something that called for some violence. His body language and facial expression made it plain that he was all too eager. The streets of the Quartieri Spagnoli were old and romantic but patrolled by young gangsters in track suits.

December 13th   Naples

I bought some books at Stazione Centrale after a long walk beside the waterfront. It was mostly Shakespeare that I felt worth purchasing. My mind now feels clear enough to read Shakespeare. I do not get an intense sense of boredom when I pick up those books anymore. I want to feel and know the common humanity of those plays and hope they help me better see such commonalities in real life.

Everything around the station was hectic. Trash was pressed against most every curb making them barely visible while cars and scooters jetted from every direction. The horns polluted the air in unison. African and Arab migrants sold random things that were laid out on the sidewalk— used shoes, old electronics, rusty kitchen utensils – nothing anyone would want. I could only imagine the best they could do was make a trade for something slightly more desirous. I overheard two Nigerians talking about going to Iran, where they said they could go to school and would have a good opportunity to get a job. As they were about to say more they turned down an empty street that would have made me seem suspicious if I followed. There were no women to be seen on the streets surrounding the station— only men hanging about.

I walked up to the Pio Monte della Misericordia behind the Duomo on the little via Tribunale to see the impressively tall Caravaggio that sits on one of its walls. *The Seven Acts of Misery* is one of his best paintings and is in very good condition. I continued further into the center on via Tribunale and everyone was flooded around the small pizza shops— so I got one, too. Two fat beggars, one a man, the other a woman, were dressed well and asked everyone for food and money. But nobody cared, especially the Italians. It seemed as though this was their corner, and they mostly targeted the tourists going in and out of the busy pizza shops. Few people idled, even those eating were on the go.

December 14th   Naples

A sudden sadness came over me today. I went to a nearby café and all the voices of all the people only made my sadness grow. I walked west along the water and the warmth of the sun and blue sky briefly minimized my sadness. I felt so hopelessly alone. There was Villa Pignatelli which I hurried into and it was pretty, its location was probably once much better, but buildings have grown in like a jungle around it. Though, it still has its place hollowed out, but just barely.

I went back out onto via Pantenope and the sky was beautiful, but my heart felt broken and I felt lost. I am so sad and angry about so many things that happened over the last two years. Just when I think I have successfully forgotten it all, those things always come back to me so suddenly. So many of the things that were said and done just continue to cut into me. I have never experienced anything like it before. It has made me so lost for so long. I am tired of thinking in generalizations about women, but at times it really feels like it is the only way to maintain a grasp on reality and some kind of logic.

I sat at a restaurant and looked out at the sun, the horizon so white and just above the sea wall on which people leaned. The waiter brought out a jug of wine of a deceiving size and I drank what was about four glasses. Then he brought out a complementary shot of Meloncello. I really hoped it was just because they were very nice and not that they were taking pity on me. It was the prettiest color and I have never tasted anything so wonderful in my life. It was like ice cream to a child. It was a new little world in a small glass that made my drunk face smile for a few moments. Sufficiently drunk at two thirty in the afternoon I slowly walked along the bay and through the piazza back to my room. Still somewhat numb from the wine though the sadness never fully subsided. I feel so lost when this feeling comes to me. I feel so lost.

December 15th   Capri

I am sitting on the terrace of my room and there is a lovely smell of fire emanating from someplace. There is a most perfect silence here. Occasionally disrupted by the small sounds of a television, the small barks of a dog or the wailing of a baby. All are too distant to be completely disruptive and they are somehow drowned out by the greater silence of the island. There is not a peep from the Mediterranean, which appears closer than it is from the center of the island where I sit. This illusion is such because there is so much of it and so little of Capri. Looking south, to my left is a steep hill and from its top down to the sea its edges shine from the fiercely bright moon and the glimmer of stars. The sky and sea are the same dark blue only separated by the slightly lighter horizon that looks like an entrance to a distant land. The sea is framed by hills on both sides.

Today I felt sick, tired and still sad and lonely with a touch of anxiety. But this place appears to be changing that sadness to happiness, the same way the presence of anything beautiful does. I figured the lack of zipping scooter noises was also playing a part in calming my soul.

The few people I interacted with on the island have been immensely pleasant. I asked a little old Italian lady for directions and she changed direction and began walking with me to show me the way. I asked a waiter about a hiking trail and he went across the street to fetch me a map and circled areas where there would be steep inclines, warning me of what to avoid and what to seek out.

My first view of the island was through the scuffed window of the ferry, and thus it took the shape and disposition of a silhouette— a tall dark mass jutting straight up like the sea had grown a breast. I did not watch the approach, so I was confronted with the presence of Capri. When I got out on the deck and caught a glimpse of the harbor and the green spotted cliffs above it felt like I was looking at a haven for people fleeing somewhere. A place that always confronts and comforts you with its beauty at every turn. There is always a beautiful view on Capri and every view of Capri is beautiful.

In this little place, the world seemed small and distant, and not worth thinking about. There is nothing to miss out there, I became sure, it is everyone not here who is missing something.

The only thing I have really read about Capri was Shirley Hazard's happy little book about Graham Greene— *Greene on Capri*. I remember smiling as I read that book in London some years ago. I barely remember much specifically but most of all the dinners they had and Greene waiting for buses back up to Anacapri. I disagreed with much of what Greene believed in and wrote but always admired his wanderlust. And now I admire it even more for all the time he spent on this beautiful rock.

December 16th   Capri

Early this morning I went for a walk towards Villa Jovis but went the wrong direction at Arco Naturale. But even when I realized I made the wrong turn I continued on my way as everything was new to me and worth discovering. Down the steep winding staircase there were some beautiful views of the northeast part of the island through the trees. As I went lower I could hear the sea more definitively and get a sense of its strength. It is not as calm as it looks from most viewpoints around the island. It is a nice illusion that Capri provides.

I kept along the path and the steep hills dotted with narrow trees leading down to the bright blue water. I searched for Casa Malaparte by investigating a little foot trail that went towards the cliff in front of the sea. A few plastic bottles made playfully into pipes and some trash littered the dead end meant for hidden parties. I got back on the path where it became a flat walkway and above me there was an abandoned villa, no longer the usual bright white of other villas on the island but spotted in a rust like color. I thought Casa Malaparte must be completely hidden from the path, but a little further along the path I looked down at the sea and it was sitting there on a peninsula that was under constant assault from the battering waves of the sea. The house looked like a beautiful red whale sleeping on a rock that could roll off at any moment back into the sea. With its color and straight lines it distinctly stood out and was clearly a foreign object. But its permanent setting is so beautiful and its simplicity of design gave it an enduring elegance. There may not be anything else on Capri the same color or even something that stands out as much, but Casa Malaparte looks like a woman wearing the brightest red dress at the fanciest party. Standing all by herself, I suppose.

I went back down to the little weathered footpath and discovered some small brick steps that turned into a concrete slope, then more narrow brick steps. Gradually I was making my way downward. The cliff edge was railed off with barbwire. At the end of the steps there was a gate covered in barbwire and locked with a rusty chain. A small sign read 'Attenti al Cane' with a little picture of a German Shepherd's head. I could more closely see the roof of Casa Malaparte. Climbing over the gate was a dangerous proposition on the steep cliff. So I turned back.

I continued along the path towards the town square and saw another downward pathway that I thought could only go to Casa Malaparte. The first step had the word 'Privato' in faded red letters painted on it. It was a curving path surrounded by trees but as it straightened out it was clear that it led directly to Casa Malaparte. There was another gate with the same 'Attenti al Cane' sign. This time it was slightly open and I considered the consequences of what I was about to do for a few moments then proceeded through the gate. I could see the red house getting closer and growing larger. The path curved inward along the cliff to the end of the little bay. There was a small newly built bridge to get over a gap in the rocks and then it was a downward straightaway to the house. I saw on the left some small brick steps that came down from where the chained and barbwire gate was. That was a more direct yet steeper descent.

There was then another gate with the same 'Attenti al Cane' sign. An open lock hung from the middle bar and the door was slightly ajar. The house looked even more beautiful through the bars of the gate. I could see the back of it, which were brick steps leading up to the roof, the white decorative and curving accent on top was peculiar, yet so different I could not help but enjoy it. I went through and could feel the force of the sea, for I was now out on the peninsula and it was similar to being on a boat or another small island off the coast of Capri.

I walked up the steps noticing the beautiful simplicity of the brickwork. From a distance they look like one large piece of an alien stone. The whole house appeared as one piece of stone. I went to the furthest edge of the house and felt the fear from the height of the cliff. It was a wild almost untouched spot. The house and all its modernity seemed like something equally wild and naturally belonged to the setting. I took in the views of each side and stood inside the white decorative piece enjoying both its unique and odd character. I knew instantly there was hardly a more beautiful spot on earth than this.

Suddenly I was startled from a young woman yelling, 'no!' The Italian woman had a look of wide-eyed horror as I was a trespasser and she likely feared for her caretaker job. In my own shock, I thought I was about to fall off the house and into the sea. 'This private!' She struggled to say in broken English. I was surprised when she initially spoke to me, but she was not threatening or intimidating and she did her best to yell at me, ordering me back up the hill. I apologized, 'scuzzi, mi scuzzi,' in my terrible Italian. I had clearly spooked her in an immense way. As I walked up the hill I felt sorry, but she was angry and walked behind me saying things in Italian mostly, 'privato, privato.' We both ran out of breath rushing up the steep hill. I began to realize just how far I walked to get there. I apologized again and hurried further up the hill. Back at the top I was thrilled with what I had seen and out of breath from both the shock and the march back up the hill. I felt sorry for scaring her. The solitude of Casa Malaparte was irresistible, its beauty seductive. There is hardly a more unique spot on earth. I walked back towards the town square along the path of grand cliffside villas facing Isole Faraglioni. It was yet another uniquely beautiful place. The islands were inspiringly large, even regal, like something only a King could own and were unreal the way they stuck out of the sea. As beautiful as the islands and the white villas that looked upon them were, they did not compare to the red beauty of Casa Malaparte.

December 17th   Capri

It was cold this morning as I sat on the lift heading up to the highest point of the island. It was a peaceful ride and the view while floating over the little homes and gardens that climb up the mountain was beautiful. One after another stone-faced Japanese tourists came down the other side passing by without noticing me except for one nice lady with a constant smile gave a happy wave. A pile of kittens rested in a sunny spot next to the operator's little office at the top of the lift.

The casual ride up was very green and made the view at the top all the more drastic and stunningly beautiful. One easily forgets the sheer height of these cliffs from being surrounded by so much green and the distant views of the sea. The shore is a long rocky way down. The sun shines so brightly on the sea it makes it into a mirror, and in some places there is not a hint of blue. The winds were strong at the top making it even chillier. There was not another soul up there. It was quite a delightful feeling to have the whole peak of the island to myself.

I decided to walk down, and it was much easier than I thought. I ran into some goats grazing on a little hill which I read is illegal here, but no one seemed to care. I took some time to sit at Villa San Michele for a little while near the Sphinx looking back at the other side of the island.

I prefer Capri town to Anacapri. It is where the buzz would be I suppose when the island is in season. Anacapri is a village. Village life is always hollow even with a view like that from Anacapri. Though I wonder about Ravello and Positano, which I will see soon enough. I found a small restaurant and had some Gnocchi Sorrentino then caught the little orange bus which rumbled round and round the steep road back down to Capri town.

I finished reading Edwin Cerro's, *The Masque of Capri*. I am interested to know a little more about Sir Hudson Lowe. Napoleon's jailer on Saint Helena. He was once in charge of the British Military on Capri while fighting Napoleon.

December 18th   Capri

It was comfortable in the shade early this morning on the steady walk up towards Villa Jovis. Lemon trees were a happy sight and there are many here inside the gates of villas that line the narrow and winding path. A garden dotted with little statues of the seven dwarves was spruced up by the presence of a Bengal cat purring in front of 'Sneezy.' The cat probably belonged to the garden's owner but wandered like a stray. Though like most of the cats I have seen here they seem well fed and at rest.

I got to the entrance of Villa Jovis and it was locked. I knew it was open Sundays but I was much too early, so I jumped the gate. The ruins were ruins and were unexciting compared to the views they looked out upon over to the Sorrento Peninsula and back at the rest of Capri and down at the sea. Walking past lemon groves and on a narrow path I again lost sight of how high up I was and was confronted with the height from the sea at the edge of the cliffs. It was simultaneously a thrill and a horrifying feeling. As I began to come down to the entrance, I walked slower thinking there might be a security guard but there was no guard. All I could see were two large dogs, something like a Mastiff, the Italian kind, slowly walking out from behind the office to the area in front of the ticket booth. Immediately, I turned around and ran back up to the top hoping the dogs would not get a sense of me or hear the jangling of keys and coins in my pockets. The dogs were large and did not look like they were there solely to bark at trespassers. With a cliff on two sides and the dogs at the front there was only one way out to avoid the dogs. I ran all the way back through the ruins until I was on the other side bordered by trees that led back towards the center of the island. I had remembered at the front gate there was a foot path leading in that direction that appeared like an off beaten trail. I had to get to that. I jumped over the wooden fence and walked on the grass through the ruins. I could barely make out the area in front of the ticket office where I had seen the dogs. I got to the edge of the woods and it was a small drop and I had to jump onto a pile of thin branches to catch myself. I had to jump another fence and then I was on the footpath. The entrance gate was open and the dogs were gone. I steadily walked down the path away from Villa Jovis still anxious from what an encounter with the dogs would have been like. There are few things more terrifying than being confronted by aggressive dogs. They are vicious and without mercy and do not let go. The air was cold and I was suddenly coughing and out of breath. Everything is a hill on Capri, and my fear of the dogs took up a lot of energy, too. My chest

My mind was in a few places because the news was of constant violence. Today, a truck drove deliberately into a market in Berlin along the Kurferstendamm. How I had thought of things like that when I walked through the Christmas Market at Alexanderplatz earlier this month. The Russian ambassador to Turkey was shot by a young off-duty police officer at an art exhibition in Ankara, and it was all caught clearly on camera. The shooter screamed about Aleppo. Three people were shot at a mosque in Zürich. Europe slowly simmers. All the footnotes are gathering— it was fitting to be looking out at a volcano.

December 20th   Sorrento

There was little reason to leave this room and the view. I sat on the balcony overlooking the bay reading Ulysses until late. It is difficult, but funny at times. It is frustrating yet there is an appeal to live in the mind of Joyce, and to try to think like him. It takes great mental strength or just a natural obsession to think as he did.

Capri has lemons and Sorrento has oranges. And I see a lot of them sitting on the street having fallen from the trees in the hills above. They go rolling down the narrow alleyways to the flat streets below.

This hotel is an ideal place to live.

December 21st   Positano

One's first view of the back side of the Sorrento Peninsula is something to remember forever. It is so beautiful it brings forth emotional excitement. There are few things more beautiful. What are the five most beautiful things in the world? I may not know all of them, but this view for sure is one of them. The sea was covered in purple and gray clouds with little patches of sunlight beaming through like spotlights on the surface of the sea. There is the thought of this is how everywhere should look and be.

Here, it is village life, mostly men are all you see. They idle, contentedly, unfazed by the beauty and are more interested in chatter. Where are the women?

Of the few people that are here, nearly everyone is a tourist. It could only be a traffic jam in the summer. Everyone packed together, forced to live a sort of vacation and village life at the same time, even on the beach.

All the couples have nothing to say to each other as they eat. Some families stay quiet, too. Only the Italians talk. Americans, Indians, English, and Japanese all stare at their plates and quietly eat their pretty food. Perhaps, there is something to what Joyce says, he puts it in the mouth of Daedalus I think, 'there is nothing more interesting than the thoughts in my head or if someone isn't saying something more interesting than the thoughts inside my head.'

I had a long and wonderful conversation on the phone last night with my father. He is deeply funny when he talks about men and their interactions with women.

A man is always guilty of sexism today. Everything a man says is sexist. So many of the fairer sex seem to be swimming in a pool of megalomania and misandry. What are we to do? Spend more time looking at Positano and not care so much, I suppose. Keep making jokes.

December 23rd   Ravello

There was no one at Villa Cimbrone. I sat on the terrace and watched the sunset. The beauty was overwhelming, and I felt a fool for not having spent thousands of days here. I sat so long that the gatekeeper forgot I was there. When I went to leave the doors were locked and I somehow pulled it open so that the large cross lock came loose. I wandered back to the piazza and up to my room. I felt drunk on the beauty of the sunset. There is so much beauty around me, it is unlike any other place and gives a feeling unlike any other. I have found contentment in places inside me that I never even knew were there.

I have seen many pictures and videos of this village and read a bit about it through avidly reading the works of Gore Vidal. This is quite a place to settle down for much of one's days to write and pontificate from. The whole place is a castle, but of course Vidal's La Rondinaia just below the Cimbrone Gardens is the best room.

December 24th   Ravello

I took pictures and selfies with some of the kids running around in little packs in front of the Church. They were rambunctious and loud. They thought I was from Germany. Firecrackers were being set off nearby every few minutes. Sometimes there were very deep booms from down in the valley between here and Scala and some big ones close to the piazza. They seem to be purely for the sound effect as there is never really any light or flash. A couple of sinister little ten-year-olds went around setting off fireworks right behind people, and some threw them at each other.

December 25th   Ravello

I watched a few minutes of the little service in the side chapel of the main church and the priest seemed like an incoherent rambler. I left and went for a walk. It is impossible to miss the Niemeyer auditorium, the top of which was peeling off. Its shape was rather dull for such a beautiful setting. I walked through the tunnel, down the hill and up to Scala. There were much less people and the feel of the village was centuries older. The church itself is over a thousand years old. One policeman stands outside the church. There was a policeman at the edge of the piazza in Ravello, too. From Scala I got a clear idea of how Ravello sits on top of a cliff with valleys on both sides. I imagined Scala and Ravello warring with one another like two little principalities. Every possible space up and down the hills is used to grow something— looks mostly like grapes.

After walking back down and around to Ravello, I found the square was a bustling and happy place with the whole village passing through. There was almost a constant scene of dozens of people kissing and hugging each other. The square was a living room for the one large family that is Ravello. After the 11:00a.m. service cleared out of the church, a band of about eight or nine men stood on the steps playing wooden horns, some equipped with sheep bags looking like Scottish bagpipers. They each wore a long black cape. The piazza was a happy and sunny little place. It was indeed Christmas in a village on top of a cliff.

December 26th   Salerno

It was a long and steep walk down to Amalfi. I think there was a more direct route, but I managed to make it on the old weathered stairs and then along the narrow roads through Atrani. Much of the route went down the seaside of Ravello. The parts of the village that are built into the cliff and covered with lemon groves. The staircases were extremely steep. One young man taking a break halfway up. The longest staircase was directly below La Rondinaia, which sits on the face of the large cliff like a floating palace. As it sweltered and I took a few moments to rest I looked up for some time and could also see the white busts on the backside of the terrace of Villa Cimbrone I had been face to face with on my first night in Ravello. I had not realized just how close the two are.

The bus ride to Salerno was nauseating and I thought of getting out at each little town we skated through. Perhaps it would be more enjoyable in a little convertible. I continually looked back at Ravello as the bus wound around the cliffs. I could more clearly see the protruding cliff and how distinctly it pops out from the rest of the mountain. The further I got from the village the more pronounced and visible La Rondinaia became. It can be seen from miles away— sometimes easier than it can be seen from Atrani or Castiglione directly below. From far away you know exactly what it is, and becomes a pedestal, where one can be admired and gazed upon. Whomever lives in such a place, certainly knows that La Rondinaia is inevitably an extension of oneself.

From nearby, it is towering above and exudes a degree of authority. It looks the perfect place from which to observe the world, for it sees what others cannot.

December 27th   Reggio di Calabria

A legion of chattering Girl Scouts with camping gear took up every seat until they got off a few stops before Paestum. The route south is dotted with cube shaped apartment buildings four or five stories high. Sometimes on their own but mostly in clumps between the sea and the tracks. They look the work of a government program and the only thing that saves them from complete ugliness are the dark orange shingles of the roofs. There is the occasional abandoned thousand-year-old structure stranded out in the field looking mature and elegant.

All the people walk slowly if at all in each town the train zips through. Italians grow from the earth and have the graceful appearance of any natural thing growing from the ground. Trees, plants. Of course we can call the women flowers. Aren't they? At some of the most random and deserted stations there was always a beautiful and elegant Italian woman standing all by herself.

Calabria is far from the rest of Italy and has the disposition of a place that its people just left or is still caught in the tangled vines of a wild society about to be discovered. There is lots of green brightened and made golden at times from the glaring presence of an afternoon sun. The Italian sun paints the lush landscape into something different every afternoon. Short and high grass is such a rich green it could have been transplanted from Ireland. The green is striking when contoured with the nearby sea. The colors have the same effect as a beautiful painting and please in the same way all good art does. There is a real happiness in this kind of green. Perhaps Ireland's abundant greenery would look the same if the skies were not so cloudy and overcast.

It is easy to find contentment in Italy, because it is a place content with itself. When you see something beautiful here it makes you think there is something else beautiful nearby. There is never a drought. There is always more to be pleased about. Nearly everything Italian becomes charming to the foreign eye. The way they always have something to say. Even the way they spit or get angry— it never appears unjustified, neurotic or out of place. The way a glass of water comes with every espresso, the way they carefully pick up a cookie or biscuit out of a display case with a small and sophisticated pair of tongues. A tall glass of milk arrives on a dish with a long spoon sticking out of it. Everything is an art in Italy. Life is an art.

I changed trains in Paola and there were a few groups of African migrants seated together on platform benches. Two charging their phones in the basement bathroom of the station. The bathroom stunk of bleach and one of the men had his charger in a plug that was on the wall just below the ceiling and he held his phone up talking on speakerphone. Migrants look out of place idling here, constantly on their phones with nowhere to go and nothing to do. They are bored with Italy and look as though they regret making the journey. There was the promise of something. A job, a house, a new and easy life. But it appears a false promise. The only safety being that of not being in a country which they consider not worth staying in, which was once called home.

The little store in the station sold cheap amateur porn DVDs and little porn booklets. One section over were religious pamphlets, books and things of the sort. Pictures of Pope John Paul II and Francesco da Paola. On the other side of the tracks were hilltop villages outlined with black clouds.

The screeching train left Paola and went through at least twenty mountain tunnels during the rest of the ride. Mountains made up much of the shoreline and short gaps of a quarter mile or so between the tunnels gave quick views of the sea or a small beach town and then we were back in the tunnel. The ride was a mix of staring at the sea and then suddenly my reflection in the window.

There was a lovely view of Sicily across the water while passing through Villa San Giovanni. The island was capped with gray clouds that were under a blue sky and the sun blaring from the south.

As Reggio di Calabria approached, Sicily was visible only through small gaps between the buildings. Reggio has a similar air to a frontier city in Patagonia. Like Punta Arenas, firmly established in the middle of nowhere. Such places feel like havens for exiles and people escaping something. It is fitting that there is a boat to Sicily, a boat to Malta or Tunisia, waiting to take you to an island or another continent.

December 28th   Reggio di Calabria

Scylla was another place locked up for the winter. A few people staring out to the horizon decorated the shoreline. The sea was the only thing making noise.

I walked through the covered walkway built into the large rock to the little marina on the other side. Rickety fishing boats piled onto the pavement next to beat up old cars. The streets narrowed the closer I got and became more charming. Doors were dressed with Christmas wreaths made of seashells. The main street is a little path that is cold and darkened like any narrow street. The sound of the sea was constant and became deeper whenever passing by little alley ways that lead down to the rocks. The water just about touches the buildings that line the shore. A deep blue in the distance, but on the rocks the water takes the color of wet snow or a soapy foam. It is like a bubbling concoction whose last ingredient is the rocks. I stood on the wet rocks and looked back at the rock of Scylla and the marina for a clear view of the village. It was a beautiful place to approach from the water, seems natural to have been included in Homer's, *The Odyssey*.

A tiled mural sits on a wall at the end of via Annunziata advertising the myth of Scylla, making sure any passerby is aware that Scylla may be small in size but not in its effect.

Having lunch at Bleu de Toi reminded me of the quiet kitsch of 'The Lobster Pot' restaurant in London I used to frequent. A place that delights because of how little it is. Holiday music played on repeat. A saxophone rendition of both Auld Lang Syne and the Dreidel song was a part of the lineup. A window framed a view of the sea and the mountains of Calabria to the north. The walls were decorated with anchors, ropes and maritime art, but unlike The Lobster Pot there were no nets or portholes. It also reminded me of a little restaurant called Kuranto in Ancud, Chile on the island of Chiloè. I wondered if little restaurants somehow all know each other.

December 29th   Reggio di Calabria

Even though it is much bigger I find Reggio di Calabria to be a more solitary and quieter place than Ravello. For such a large place to have so few people on the streets is confusing. The one main glittering pedestrian street was filled the other night, but now the people are all gone, during both day and night. A restaurant or a pizza place is full, but there are so few people anywhere else it is as if they have fled. Cafés have only a straggler or two.

There is something I like about this city. I put it down to location. Sicily is in the distance. There is a port nearby, another port only a couple miles away at Villa San Giovanni. Reggio is a crossroads. Here you feel hope, you feel there is possibility and there is choice. You get a sense of freedom. Any direction seems like a good option. It is easy to be filled with the anticipation of Sicily.

December 30th   Taormina

I finally finished Ulysses. I will have to read it seven more times to fully comprehend it, but I assume that is Joyce's hope for us all. It beautifully ends with, the word "yes." A relief to have some brevity after nine hundred pages.

Arriving by boat is the most pleasant way to arrive. Short boat rides are always pleasant. They always remind me of others I have taken. Cape Town to Robben Island. Colonia to Buenos Aires. And most recently Naples to Capri. It is like crossing a border even if it is the same country, and you are not filled with the extended anxiety of a long boat ride where there is always a sense of wondering if the boat will make it.

Sicily already feels familiar as I see names of places that are the last names of people I have met or known, Nizza, Policastro, and Scala. In Reggio I was only a few miles from Lazzaro, the last name of a friend of mine and a town which is at the uttermost end of the mainland. On the train from Messina I took note of the station names Alì Terme and Letojanni because of their spelling. Mount Etna is covered in clouds and the view of the sea is beautiful.

In Naples, I read *The Leopard* by Giuseppe Tomasi di Lampedusa and it made me eager to be here. Especially from a paragraph noting how Sicilians are '…old, very old,' and are always dealing with the weight of other civilizations conquering the island. Lampedusa goes on to mention how Sicilians are as white as any other European yet have been a colony for centuries, which has had an exhausting effect.

From reading this sentence in the premier novel about the island, I wondered what Sicily would become with more migrants from Africa and the

Middle East, who are largely non-white. But I did not think too much about it as Sicily will likely remain the same for the most part as it has taken the shape of a stopping off point for those coming as a migrant, refugee or as a tourist. *The Leopard* continues with many more brilliant lines and descriptions of Sicilians. None better than when stating that invaders are trying to teach Sicilians good manners, which is never a success as Sicilians think they themselves are gods. They never want to improve, because they consider themselves to be perfect and all they wish to have is sleep, precious sleep, which is a fixation with death.

What will happen while they sleep? Probably nothing. And this hankering for oblivion sounds like a people unafraid of death. I read it as a way to say that Sicilians live well. Vanity certainly goes a long way in creating a beautiful civilization in some respects, and for Sicilians perhaps it has been a successful method of perseverance.

My first taste of food in Sicily was memorable. Leaving the little restaurant felt like leaving a phenomenal concert. The Caponata and Spaghetti al Limone both came with grated pistachios. It was a dramatic performance.

Nearly every bustling street scene outside of Rome is decorated by men and the sounds of fireworks set off by little sinister boys. But here my first thought was always that they were gunshots.

December 31st   Taormina

The walk up the winding roads to Castel Moro was not as strenuous as I thought. The sky was bright and every step meant a cooling of the temperature. There was a beautiful view of Etna covered in snow with a steady flow of smoke emanating from its peak. Together the sea and snow occupied the same view and I was pleased to realize that this strange pairing was normal on this island.

The walk down the front side of the hill was a breeze and I was soon back into the center of town. I relaxed at a café on the main square listening to the old men playing Frank Sinatra, 'Volare,' and 'Lazy Mary' on their little guitars. Old couples got up and slow danced in between tables at the outdoor café. This is how a year ends.

January 2nd   Catania

A much fuller stream of smoke puffed out of Etna towards the sea this morning. One cannot help but feel a touch of both anxiety and excitement. I took a taxi down to the station and the roads were as winding and nauseating as those on the Amalfi coast, all the while the view was spectacular.

German and French tourists gathered at the train station café sipping espresso and wine in little homogenous groups. The delayed train gave me more time to look at the serene sea between the columns of the platform bridge. The columns and roof framed a view worthy of more than a glance. There is almost always a view of the sea from anywhere in Taormina. One need not think of wanting to be content, for contentedness happens without achieving, acquiring or consuming anything. Taormina constantly presents you with calmness. There was something in the gentle wind that gave a sense of relaxation. It is as though I am a part of the "sleep" that Lampedusa speaks of about Sicilians. There is no such thing as boredom here. Doing nothing is a part of life. How enjoyable it is, to be; in Sicily.

It is much warmer than the previous two days. I have been carrying a sniffle which has subsided somewhat after a couple pots of tea this morning. It has been a nice quiet few days at the San Domenico Palace, filled with peaceful walks in the garden and the small inner courtyard that also has some greenery, as well as hanging out on the terraces looking out at the volcano and the sea. This past year has tired me out in lots of ways and brought on far too much cynicism. I have met far too many people in the past two years that have made me squeamish. New York seems full of them. People come from everywhere to that city to let their mess out. People use others in New York like oxygen tanks.

Catania is so spread out it feels there are only thirty thousand people instead of three hundred thousand. The white of the Duomo glitters in the sun as if it were gold. The black stone of the buildings makes it medieval and more suited to a colder setting in say France or Holland. It must be dreadfully hot here in the summer, that is why the black stone is confounding. Most end up in the piazza near the lovely elephant statue to eat fried things from the sea while overlooking Osteria Marina. As the workers clean up, the seagulls swarm over the entirety of the market in a beautiful and chaotic hysteria. Then in an orderly military fashion they become a synchronized flock and jet like a school of fish around the corner of a building. Only to return a minute later devolved back into airborne chaos.

Some of the small side streets are dirty but the hand-laid stone and the buildings makes for a charming antidote. The fruit and vegetables that sit outside of little shops are bright and more appetizing than I have ever seen before. They are colorful jewels stacked by people who appreciate them as much as jewelers do precious rocks. And shouldn't they be considered that? It made the fried calamari I had just eaten near the market seem like trash.

I was at a restaurant tonight having Penne with crushed pistachios and one of the waiters— a heavyset man with a full head of thick curly black hair, in a black vest, white shirt and a silk scarf bunched up around his neck— started to sing classic Italian-American songs. Along with, 'My Way,' 'Volare,' and 'That's Amore.' He had a small amplifier and speaker on wheels and took tips in a cat shaped piggy bank.

January 3rd   Catania

I was wandering in poorer neighborhoods this morning. People young and old know an outsider when they see one and I, with my stocking cap so low it almost covered my eyes was on the receiving end of longer than usual stares. Young fat kids in sweat suits gave a territorial look as they worked like grown men unloading crates of fruit and bags of concrete. Staring back as they walk in the other direction down an alley.

People casually litter, peanut shells and orange peels but also napkins discarded into the street or dropped behind them as they move about. It is clear who is Sicilian and who is not. Almost every building is covered in clothing, sheets and towels flowing gracefully in the wind hanging out to dry. A sign of a working-class neighborhood I suppose or perhaps of a place unwilling to change.

The west of the city is mostly quiet and industrial. The only noise came from a scrap metal yard. A large excavator with a six-finger claw— ripped all kinds of rusted metal and junk from the forty-foot-high pile and into a crusher. A man in a little old beat up red hatchback drove through the gate and out the back he spilled out a large heap of scrap along with a car engine. The excavator elegantly grabbed the engine, gently placing it on a nearby table for inspection.

Wherever there are people they are men hanging outside of garages or butcher shops. Women are a rare sight and even rarer to be seen without the company of a man. Some baboonish men hang around beside a butcher shop where half of a four hundred-pound-pig hangs from a hook under a tent. Nearby the smell of charcoal emanates from a long rectangular grill. None of the men work, but simply wait for the pig to be cooked.

It was still early when I circled back to the fish market and witnessed all the beauty of the bustling bazaar, wet and adorned with fish and shouting men. The silvery scales of fish shine in the sun and change colors as you move along. Octopus slowly slide their legs while shrimp wiggle about. Some of the men were pushy in their selling technique, shouting, 'pesce, pesce, pesce.' Old men sporadically dip their hands in a bucket and flick the water on to all of their fish. At the edge of the market near the piazza there are more fishmongers hacking away at large swordfish with medieval machetes. Blades about two feet long and six or seven inches tall— the end is a dull vertical edge rather than an elegantly rounded one, they appear to have been recently hacked off of a large piece of steel.

The noise of the market often flares, and one expects a scuffle to arise somewhere in the scrum of people. The sellers know they are on stage and are graceful, never pretentious or catering to anything but selling fish.

One seller, probably in his fifties, bald with white hair around the sides of his head— the peak of his tanned head is adorned with saggy wrinkles— like he had been given an extra bunch of skin. I could not imagine the man as a child. It looks as though he was born with a bald spot. He lost his patience with a young assistant and like an elder gorilla he swatted at the young man's hoodie-covered head, before motioning around a bit more with the same swatting hand. He then spoke to his customer and gave the man gentle kisses on both cheeks.

The minor characters are the wandering herb sellers slowly walking up the aisles holding parsley and cilantro but selling very little. Vegetable stalls have better luck with beautiful arrangements of artichokes and are all busy. One seller casually broke off pieces of an onion to snack on them like potato chips.

Half corpses of lamb, whole cow livers and kidneys glistened on white chopping blocks. Off-white sets of intestines hung like chandeliers at the front of stalls seemingly more for decoration than for sale.

January 4th   Syracuse

The short train ride was enjoyable and along the way I caught occasional glimpses of the shiny sea as I glanced up from reading about the Vandals and the Byzantines in a history of Sicily. I am currently at the Muslims and then it is on to the Normans. But the Sicilians are still in love with their Greek-ness thus far in the book, and are now speaking Latin.

The names of some Sicilian cities originate from the Arabic of their former Muslim rulers;

Marsala is mars-al-allah— Port of Allah
Caltanissetta is kalat an-mis— Castle of women

The market in Syracuse is a much more subtle place than the one in Catania. Andrea Borderi and his little sandwich shop gives it almost all of its life and excitement. He is a happy man making beautiful sandwiches with four or five kinds of cheese and various other ingredients. The ladies working beside him hand out cheese, and bread covered in cheese to everyone who waits on the slow-moving line. Andrea smiles and gives me a fist bump when I order mine with mortadella. The taste of some of the cheeses was unreal and something I will always remember. I have never had anything like them. One bite was all the taste one would need for an entire meal.

Just by looking at a map of the city I knew it would be beautiful. Cities by the sea are like that, but Syracuse is especially beautiful. There is a maturity to Syracuse, of course for its ancientness but also its location. Half of the city being an island— known as Ortygia, is in a position almost too good to be true, where the streets narrow and become the cool places that one finds in a charming French mountain village. But the sea is never far and appears framed by close knit buildings. I cannot help but think of the cold and slush of New York at the moment. Not only does it induce misery but from this vantage point also appears a foolish place to be.

I forgot to see the two Caravaggio paintings in Messina, but when I thought of the one here I happened to be standing right in front of the church where it hangs. *The Burial of Saint Lucy* is a peculiar painting and certainly unique compared to other Caravaggio paintings I have seen from Rome down to here. Much of the *Saint Lucy* painting is nearly blank, the people are much more faded, and no part of them jumps off the canvas like so many other people depicted by Caravaggio. The church does not let anyone take photos nor do they let anyone near the painting even though it hangs on a wall about fifteen feet off the ground. The rope stretched in front of the altar kept everyone nearly thirty feet away. I believe the painting was done in haste and I wonder if it was done solely by Caravaggio without assistance of any kind. Perhaps that partly is the cause of the haste and thus the resulting style. Individuals have little time for detail, though assistants do have the time. Some paintings make you want to steal them: I get that feeling with much of Caravaggio's work, he inspires dark instincts. There was something about this one that makes me want it all to myself and I would not be bothered going to great lengths to have secret doors and false walls in a house to keep it all to myself.

January 5th   Syracuse

I spent much of the day walking amongst the ruins beside the city. I could not help but linger for some time to listen to the echo of hooting pigeons inside the Ear of Dionysus. I tested out the acoustics of the cave myself with a few comical shouts. It was early enough and no one else had ventured into the ruins. There is something intriguing about that cave. Not least because it was given its name by Caravaggio. Caves somehow take the shape of a living organism. Like an oversized clam or oyster.

The wind was very strong on the west side of Ortygia. The waves were choppy. The beauty of the sea caused me to lose track of time and thus it received much of mine.

Today I read that when Columbus first saw Cuba he wrote in his journal, 'October 28, 1492, "all the country is high like Sicily."'

January 7th   Ragusa

I knew it would be a long day. My attempt to go to Malta was thwarted when I was nearly at the port in Pozzallo. The notice in the window of the Virtu Ferry building said the one ferry that day was canceled due to weather. It was all the more frustrating as there was no weather in sight, just a beautiful Mediterranean sky and a calm sea.

I started in Syracuse and took the three-car train down to Noto. A pretty little town on a hill. A massive cathedral at the center with SPQR over the doorway was a surprising sight in such a small town. A sleeping giant. Outside the main drag the town was nearly empty— sometimes there were groups of men socializing outside a café but would soon disperse or go inside leaving the streets deserted once again. Pairs of boys roamed narrow streets, talking loudly with their deep voices that could be mistaken for grown men— echoing off the buildings.

I looked into the windows of a Tabacchi shop that had books in the window. They were displayed with high regard. Books are the highest art. To have a book is to have someone else's thoughts with you. To be with that person. And to live with books is to be surrounded by the best people that have ever lived. I failed to find a book worth purchasing and left after purchasing a pack of gum. So much for my praising of books, I thought.

Along the train line were groves, groves and more groves. If it was not an orange grove it was a lemon grove. Perfectly symmetrical groves that were much thicker than the others I had seen so far. The regular presence of cacti set against a mostly green landscape makes for surreal viewing. A much-welcomed overdose of green.

I should have known there would be no chance of getting to Malta— it all seemed too easy. Why would a boat be on time or go at all? What an ordeal it is to get a boat to anywhere. I often thought it would be a short easy ride like the one from Reggio to Messina, but it was much further. I slightly remembered seeing a weather report for Malta that it would be windy. I realize from this spot just how isolated and forgotten Sicily is. There appears little reason for things to run on time or go as planned. Things happen when something great wills it so.

I was stuck in Pozzallo and did not feel like being there nor did I want to go to Malta anymore. Even though I really wanted to see the Caravaggio paintings there, which was my only reason in the first place. I did not want to spend a whole day waiting around Pozzallo for a boat. Pozzallo looks out to the prettiest view of the sea, and the freighters sit on the horizon that appears to be above you. So you almost look up at the boats. While the sun was out it was much warmer than both Noto and Syracuse, but the cold air quickly returned when it darkened. I was stuck waiting around for the train which no one else was doing. No one took the train. Just me and a handful of day trippers. But now it was night. The train to Noto and to Pozzallo was a funny one-car-train that had a dual air of exclusivity and primitiveness. I bought meat, cheese, bread and some chocolate at the nearby supermarket for three euros. The station was locked, and the lights were on over the tracks only making it seem more hopeless and isolated amongst the abandoned area on the other side. A rickety loudspeaker announced, 'retarde,' several times and I started to think, what am I doing here? I could be anywhere. But I am here in this empty train station that no one uses, standing in the dark, in the cold, chewing on a baguette. This was one of the dead ends of travel. Everything felt like a failure in that moment. The thought of going to an airport and taking as many flights as one needs to get closer to home lingers in the mind, just for the thought of doing something that moves at a greater speed. I was supposed to be getting on a boat to a beautiful island off the coast of another beautiful island in the sea. But I was here trying to go inland to Ragusa.

I gave up on the train and spoke to some fruit sellers who lingered in their truck outside the grocery store. I asked them to call me a taxi and they kindly did so. While we waited we talked about how many Sicilians there are in America.

The taxi drove at a speed unlawful almost anywhere, but there were only a few cars on the road which provided a facade of safety as there were less people to crash into. The further inland we went the lower the temperature dropped, and I felt even more hopeless. The driver, Franco, told me how I really should go to Malta— 'the girls! The women! Malta is beautiful.' He loved Malta more than Sicily. I wanted to tell him to stop reminding me of Malta, but his enthusiasm was distracting me from the cold and his reckless driving. The winding road in the dark looked like it was leading to another dead end, but I was consoled by the fact that we were making so much ground so quickly and getting closer to Ragusa. Going fast somewhere was preferable to standing in the cold for so long and going nowhere. We were going up and down hills and as Franco played with his phone and talked to me while driving, I thought we were certain for a wreck with cars that came around blindsides, but he would casually swerve somehow not crashing into anything.

The dead end of Pozzallo had filled me with loneliness. The socializing groups of kids did not look appealing. It was a loneliness that came out of something not going right in this dark winding road in the countryside. I only felt more uncertainty. I also felt dread at the dropping of the temperature. The cold was something I have been trying to avoid for two years. The temperatures in New York were in the twenties and intermittently got close to below zero. Franco would regularly point out that it was getting closer to below freezing the closer we got. I was tired for I had probably walked close to ten miles and was ready to tell Franco to take me to Syracuse. I knew nothing of the road in front of us. It only felt like more loneliness. But we turned around a bend and the lights of Ragusa Ibla were all I could see and all I needed to see to know I was in the right place.

January 8th   Ragusa

I took a seat during mid-morning mass at the Duomo amongst the happy little crowd of worshippers including a man nearly seven feet tall alongside his young son only an inch or two shorter. Lots of music, pleasant songs, and a few times the piano played long after the singing was done and continued as background for some of the prayers.

It was much lighter inside than any cathedral I had ever seen because of the large windows of the dome. It made every other church and cathedral seem like a dark cave. It was cold this morning especially before the sun had time to get high over all the city walls to the narrow streets and stairways. It must help the little streets stay cool in the heat of summer. As I sat in the service the sweat from my head soaked onto my clothes and I started to get a chill.

The priest took some time getting the Eucharist ready even with the assistance of the altar boys in their white robes adorned with two vertical orange stripes. The long quiet pause was only interrupted by the sound of a few elderly people taking their seats. Pews, no matter how new, always seem to squeak and wobble. After the long pause, the service continued and the people lined up. What an ordeal, I thought. Then I remembered what an ordeal it was for me to get here.

I find it too cold in Ragusa, even during daylight— a few degrees warmer would make it more pleasant, but unfortunately those degrees are elsewhere. Everyone made their way to the pretty garden at the far end of Ragusa Ibla. The green of the tropical trees in the blue sky was deceiving of warm weather, the sun only added to the deception. The palm trees were groomed nearly to the top. One loan palm tree was groomed completely of its palms— and sat there, bald, in a unique aesthetic.

The temperature peaked around 12:30pm, then suddenly retreated. The same goes for people in the little street. They retreat to restaurants for lunch and Ragusa is empty.

Sunday is significant not just because it is a holy day or because it is a day of rest. There are so few people outside or at work in the tourist shops, it appears as a day not just to rest, but a day to not even be seen. Is everyone at home or did they leave town altogether? So many places so far have been like that on Sundays. Even in narrow streets where one presumably can hear much conversation coming from little houses, there are no sounds at all.

I think I will go to Caltanissetta tomorrow. I am aware it is a dull town, but I have to eventually get to Palermo which I am eager to see. I also want to get to Agrigento. The temperature in Enna is around twenty degrees Fahrenheit. I do not think it is worth it in this weather.

I get the feeling everyday will feel like Sunday in the center of Sicily.

January 9th   Messina

I gave up on trying to go across the island this morning after the train and its replacement buses failed to show up. I guess I had no choice. It was getting colder and the only reliable mode of travel was my feet. It feels like southern Sicily aims to keep people away by making it difficult to get anywhere. Who can blame them? I wasted too much time trying to go in that direction and was happy to be on the bus heading to Catania. A peculiar number of young Sicilian men with a red beard dotted the seats of the bus, and I double checked with one if I was indeed getting on the correct bus. With a lyrical 'Si,' he told me I was going the right way and soon enough I was happily traveling along the warm sunny coast beneath Taormina. The sides of train tracks were covered in patches of melting snow while the sea looked warm and inviting. Etna in the distance looked like something from Alaska.

The ride to Catania was interesting for the landscape had several gum drop hills as one would see in the Welsh countryside, spotted with ruined stone walls. Nearly every field was decorated with a crumbling stone structure from centuries ago. There were some junkies waiting at the end of village roads for a ride. Dirty prostitutes in the countryside with worn-out faces.

The thought of being stuck fills me with dread. It bothers me so much when I am stuck in a place, even one as pretty as Ragusa. Movement is what gets me through a day. Sometimes the thought of sitting is so objectionable I have to simply stand and walk about the room in which I am staying. Perhaps these empty places are beginning to feel emptier to me. I am only completely comforted by cities as far as places are concerned. I try to trick myself into believing there is something in these far-out places. I should stick to what I know makes me happiest.

I was sad again today. Out of nowhere, which makes my thoughts spiral, and I think of all those things that bothered me so much for so long. It is forever unresolved, and I am left with the permanent hole in my heart and a nagging grip around my throat. Sometimes it all becomes a blur which helps because I cannot focus on any one thing specifically. More fool me for trying to be around people. I think of Flaubert's Dictionary which defined people as the, "cause of all problems." Let us listen to Flaubert. And never forget his words.

There was a tremendous sky above the marina and the Strait of Messina today. Some clouds were nearly black— some parts of the sea were nearly black, too. The sun made a perfect spotlight onto a section of Reggio di Calabria in the distance. A blue sky and white clouds were visible far north towards Scylla.

I started reading Daphne Phelps', *A House in Sicily*, and I underlined the passage, "many women will work happily for a man, but I hate being 'under' a woman." I found Taormina even more appealing when Phelps wrote, "People become eccentric in those far out places."

I found out I may have to go to Naples tomorrow or the next day to get legal documents notarized at the US Consulate. Something to do with taxes. Of course, the consulate in Palermo is closed. That would have been too easy. No matter how hard one may try, paperwork is impossible to escape.

January 10th   Messina

Coming back from the museum this morning, I saw the most beautiful and elegant woman on the train. She was about forty with light brown hair. Everything about how she dressed was done perfectly. The boots, there was something decidedly sophisticated about the tall boots on her petite frame or at the bottom of her petite frame. Like they were one of a kind. She was youthful and mature at the same time. A woman in two places. I glanced to see if she was older or younger than I thought, but I could not figure out or decide which. When I looked at her face the name of the city came to my mind. Messina. When the train arrived at her stop she flew away like a bird from a cage.

I did not care much for the *Adoration of Shepherds*, but loved very much the oversized '*Resurrection of Lazarus.*' Its title is much more beautiful in Italian, *Risurrezione di Lazzaro*. So even and smooth is the paint, it looks printed onto the canvas. In an old little room shaped like a squashed pentagon— with three cameras staring down at me and no other visitor, the security guard stayed about five to ten feet behind me the whole time but left me alone in the little Caravaggio room.

I smiled when I saw that much of the top half of the *Risurrezione* is nearly all black— which brought me to think more about *The Burial of Saint Lucy*, in

Syracuse. The *Risurrezione* would be much more enjoyable in a similar setting as the *Saint Lucy*. I found something daring about all that black space. It can be easily criticized as being simple, but in truth it puts a great deal of pressure on the rest of the painting.

Palermo

I am very happy to be here. And happy I do not have to backtrack or fly to Naples. The paperwork was resolved without me or my signatures. How, I am not sure, and do not wish to know.

The train ride along the coast was pleasant. The sea was a much lighter blue, I can only imagine it to be even better in the summer and under a shining blue sky. There were lots of small rocks that jutted upwards out of the water to form miniature islands not too far from the shore. Two dumb birds sitting on one rock, stared back at the train. It was a peculiar place to sit, seemingly stranded as if they were unable to fly. The train at times rides right along the edge of a small cliff above the sea enabling you to look straight down at the water. The Aeolian Islands are visible on the horizon for most of the ride.

As rain softly drizzled onto my forehead, I walked down via Maqueda all the way to the new city and saw how quickly the city changes from old to new. Lots of people from Africa, Sri Lanka, and India worked the shops in the old part of the city. The new city feels

Parisian in character and at times even grander than the new sections of Rome.

January 11th   Palermo

Via Maqueda is an odd street. There is something almost comical about how long it is and yet both ends are marked by the side of a mountain framed by buildings on each side. It is lined with some of the dirtiest of buildings. Aesthetically, it is a street that takes some getting used to. Its intersection with Corso Vittorio Emanuele, which forms a beautiful little piazza, Quattro Canti, or Piazza Vigilena— is decorated with four buildings that have almost identical façades adorned with statues and fountains. All of the façades are covered in dirt. The piazza and the two large streets are oddly lacking in traffic. The gloomy gray sky is a dirty ceiling making the street look like a tunnel. To add to the peculiarity of via Maqueda, an army truck slowly creeped down the street towards the train station at a pace less than those walking nearby.

Palermo, mostly in the older part of town there is an ugly, dark and generally old feel to everything. Even the separated chimes of church bells release a sense of doom through the air. They almost warn one to be careful, not to be too hopeful or perhaps not to overstay your welcome.

I quickly put the Chiesa Capitolare di San Cataldo into my list of favorite buildings. This charming little church on top of the old city wall is so playful looking I consider it a living thing. In the shape of a tall gift box decorated with its three fading red domes makes it seem as though its architect was having a little fun. But, so I have read, it has the sort of characteristics attributed to Islamic and Norman influences and some as far as England and France. The symbol with five crosses on the doors and curtains inside looks like that of a secret society and I felt that much mystery was added to the church by finding out that it is often used privately.

Across the piazza, the Chiesa di Santa Caterina had the most peculiar spiraling columns just inside the door resembling the color of uncooked veal. Carvings and frescoes covered nearly every space. Oddities abound. There were dozens of statues and busts of children. Sometimes just a head poking out off a wall at a seemingly random height. There must have been some sort of religious pattern to the carvings which I could not follow, but it looks as though the artisans were given carte blanche with some things yet told to stick to certain colors. Many of the faces have odd or strained expressions, very few are happy— many in anguish or horrified, perhaps from pain. Near the altar there was an echo from the ghostly meowing of cats. Sometimes it seems as though they were up on the second floor. I could not tell whether they were dying or just making noise for the sake of it, perhaps both. Outside on the stone railings back down into the piazza I noticed some funny little steel hooks hammered on to the stone that were bent down nearly flat and could give an unpleasant surprise to someone's hand.

I naturally made my way to the Mercato di Bolaro. There was lots to please the eye and some to displease it at times. Most everything was wet after the morning drizzle but even more so from the fish and meat juices navigating the cracks between the ground's stones.

One man had lifted a large stone from the ground and started to bucket out overflowing water to another drain. When I walked by a little later he was attempting to work on what looked like the most medieval piping system I had ever seen.

The market was relatively quiet at noon, many had come and gone. Sellers did not shout or tout their goods— there was a quiet order to the messy place. Though, the people were Nigerian and Sri Lankan and of course Sicilian, everyone looked from the same neighborhood and on the same page. Never was there an argument or any bargaining. I tried some fried eggplant, a hard cheese, almost like Feta and covered in caramelized onions. I got a bag full of olives and capers and wandered around. The area behind the market was an absolute mess covered in trash and crumbling buildings that looked like they had once or twice been under siege by an invading military. Everyone looked at me suspiciously as I passed by, Italians and Nigerians knowing I did not belong there. The university building beside a piazza had a third of a tattered Italian flag hanging from its façade and two-thirds of an EU flag. Cats ate out of piles of abhorrent trash piles beside dumpsters, in which there were dozens of syringes. A man walking his dog off the leash followed behind as the dog sniffed through the same pile of trash. It was a gangland ghetto, if it was not the Italian mafia then it was the Nigerian mafia. Young confident and always skinny Nigerian boys walked with staggering confidence, afraid of nothing. Violence did not seem far. It was not a place for any sort of outsider. When I got back to the edge of the market I stopped at a little panini stand where the smell of ham cooking in its own fat sizzled on a little grill. The only customer was a short middle-aged lady. Just before I was about to say something to the guy cooking, another guy sitting at the store shouted out one word I could not understand that could only have been aimed at me. Ugly, fat and about thirty, he stared deeply at me with a deadened face, said nothing and quickly made two sideways snaps of his head, indicating I was not welcome. His chin only moved about an inch before snapping back to the center. It was a most unnatural way to move one's head— it was clear and none too difficult to realize that he was telling me to move on, which I swiftly did without any fuss.

He made what I was thinking about the market the whole time become glitteringly clear. That it was controlled. Everything was for a reason. I walked around the stalls a little more but there was now a dark air to the place and I found my way back to the via Maqueda, which now seemed a glittering boulevard in comparison to the market. The difference between Palermo and Rome or even Naples was dark. I understood much better why Italy is more than one country. Why Sicily is really its own country governed by local kings as they wish and their kind of order rules the street no matter who is officially in charge. The presence of so many Nigerians could only be possible because of some sort of Nigerian gang presence and a compromise or deal with the local mafia. There is no room for outsiders who do not compromise.

Somewhat dazed and feeling lucky to have been only given a dirty look, I was relieved to be on via Maqueda and via Roma. I felt I had made it out unscathed. I could not imagine going there at night. There was not one car anywhere in sight or near the market. The only way in or out was on foot.

I made my way to the little Oratorio di San Lorenzo. Along the way there was a small street sign in Italian, Hebrew and Arabic. At the Oratorio there was a pretty little courtyard beside the little chapel that now held a replica of the stolen Caravaggio nativity painting. After being in the market and this little neighborhood it seems only fitting that the painting had been stolen in 1969, my only wonder was why it took till 1969 for it to be stolen from this vulnerable little place. The new painting indeed looked new and I stood as close as I could, noticing the two small balconies on each side which the thieves must have climbed up onto. After seeing the other Caravaggio paintings in Syracuse and Messina I was surprised at the size of this one. I had thought it was much larger and thus only adding to the difficulty of stealing it. But since it was cut out it did not seem far-fetched for it to be rolled up and carried out. The girl who sold me a ticket stood in the chapel with me the whole time to make sure I did not take a picture of the reproduction painting that was only a year old.

It would not surprise me if the reproduction was stolen, too. Just to let everyone know who is in charge.

January 12th   Palermo

It is fitting that the artist who painted the *Triumph of Death* fresco at the Palazzo Abatellis remains unknown. Surely it was someone madly talented. Anyone that looks at death in the way expressed by the artist certainly possesses an abundance of maturity. The description in a little write up nearby said, "death spares those who recognize and invoke him but strikes those who are unaware of the approaching doom and think they are sheltered by vain rules, principles and conventions."

I was messaging with my cousin Andy about the fresco and I mentioned how old it was, and he replied, "death been around for a long time."

It was in good enough condition, but still badly damaged, and large sections have broken off. Perhaps it is lucky to still be here after all this time and to have escaped complete ruin during the bombing raids of World War II. It seems as though those World War II bombs were just about everywhere.

Via Maqueda is a much more pleasant street in the evening and entirely pedestrian. The dirtiness of the buildings is shaded by the night and the street is lit by cheerful lamps that stretch on forever in both directions. People stroll calmly as if in a garden or courtyard. Never are there too many people.

A beautiful girl sat next to her boyfriend eyeing me as I ate my pizza and eyed her back. The boyfriend took notice of me as they left. Precious little nothings.

Sometimes I like to pour out the contents of the small bag I travel with onto the bed and then get under the sheets. Some of it is next to me and some scattered on me as I sleep. A mischievous feeling, that makes no sense, and no bedmate would approve of.

One time I got into a girl's bed, on 39th Street, and while she was in the bathroom I struggled with the sheets that were tucked way too tight into the mattress. I ripped them all up out of the mattress bringing it all onto the top of the bed, partially balled up. As she came out of the bathroom and got into bed, she could not understand what had happened to the sheets. She kept saying: "what happened," over and over. I said, "I don't know, let's not worry about it, let's just go to sleep."

Sometimes when I stay at a hotel for an extended period of time I get so comfortable and in such a relaxing routine that I feel it would be acceptable to wander down to the lobby without any clothes on. I must keep hold of my senses.

January 15th   Palermo

The day started pleasantly enough after I read a beautiful line in D'Annunzio's *Pleasure,* which describes a woman who has the complexion of 'light, roses, and milk,' and can only be seen on babies depicted in the paintings of Reynolds, Gainsborough, and Lawrence. It is such a beautiful book, that almost every sentence has some rich element worthy of taking note.

I am planning on going by train to Agrigento tomorrow morning, but I do not know if it will happen. I feel incredibly lost at the moment. It is all my fault. I do not know what to do. A part of me wants to be in New York, because of its distractions, or I guess

Rome or Florence. The small towns and the countryside are leaving me hollow. I cannot fill those places up, nor can they fill me up sufficiently. There is no mystery to them. They are just empty. That is it. Only cities are comforting. There is always something there, even in the most foreign places.

I have spent a few nights in Palermo and it is a rather tame city. Last night, Saturday, the streets were crowded but few were rambunctious or rowdy. Just happy. There is no madness— not a single drunk person.

The food is a little odd here. Of course there are many restaurants, but there are so many people who prefer eating street food. Simple things like puffy pizzas, Arrancine balls, fried chickpea chips, croquettes or cannoli. Almost everyplace has the exact same things. Whenever I, myself had something to eat in my hand as I walked on the street, idlers and passersby would take a good long look at whatever it was. I find more people generally looking at me, too. I must look very different, very white, very foreign to Sicilians, and obviously a foreigner. Sicilians seem so stirred by that, not in any threatening way. Perhaps it reminds them of who they are, or they just do not want anyone to disturb their "sleep."

I realize my solitude is not so enjoyable all the time— it is not always something to love and seek— though sometimes it is. It is often a place of failure. A failure with people, a dissatisfaction with people, and a rejection of people. I love people and I wish it were an easier road with them. That is why I love a city. The possibility of people are there. The more small places I go to the more I realize how isolated and solitary those people are. It is frightening. But I guess two people can be a crowd no matter where you are.

I am starting to miss New York, but I must stay away for another month or two. I just have to go to some more big cities. I wonder what New York will be in five days. Trump will be president. Change of some sort seems inevitable. What will happen to New York? Probably nothing? As long as they let me below Houston Street, I do not care much. It will make me happy to go from this exile to that exile.

I have misplaced my stocking hat. I was under the illusion it could never be lost. I guess that is how one thinks when traveling with so few things. Now I will be cold in Agrigento, too. I hope they sell some near the station.

January 16th   Messina

As the train left Palermo, some beautiful green hills could be seen behind ugly apartment buildings—jutting up into the sky. The other side was a view of the sea and the prettiest clouds sat atop the horizon. As the train turned inland after Termini Imerese there were an endless number of hills, like they were piled up against one another for miles and miles. They stood out, for they were not simply a slope in the landscape but were full of character and dramatic color. They were not just slopes of grass, but often rocky inclines covered mostly in grass and trees. So much green covered the rock that it looked as though it was the rocks that were growing out of the grass. The center of Sicily is what the center of an island should be. Vastly different from its coast, magical, odd, difficult—fairytale-like. There was an undoubtedly winter sky with the presence of the clouds covering most of the sky, playing tricks with the light trying to shine its way through. In some places the sky was black while the sun came from far away to shine brightly on a hill underneath. Green grass became lime green and yellow green. The further inland the train went the more full of character the landscape became.

Random patches of trees sat isolated on a cultivated hillside while a single solitary tree was somehow on the top of a hill. Why there? Looking like a birthmark or a mistake.

There were muddy cracks winding through the countryside and seem to exist because of some sort of mudslide or trembling shift in the earth's interior structure. The banks of the creeks are sometimes five to ten feet high and freshly fallen into the muddy water. A muddy stream is an unpromising sight. It conveys a primitive nature and reminded me of being on the Mekong River, the murkiest water I have ever seen. Where do muddy rivers end?

Ghostly farmhouses with black, rectangular windows sat in the middle of farms. I did not see one person working in the fields the entire ride. I think I only saw two or three people the whole way. Perhaps it was too early. Perhaps all that food grows and picks itself after all those centuries of the same process. That would be unfair to the people that actually work the land. But this land looks mature or perhaps it is just asleep. The hilly and jagged countryside continued and the white and gray clouds became a kind of mist as they touch the tops of the hills and rocky peaks. Some hills were covered in rocks that could be picked up with one hand. Like they had been deliberately scattered about. Other hillsides had piles of boulders that could only be the work of a machine or dynamite but there was no good reason for their position from where I sat. I resigned myself to thinking that time put them there. The panoply of green continued. There were dozens of greens. From Olive to Kelly. A large green hill would have a huge rock formation bulging out the top. Of course there was the presence of the abandoned and crumbling stone structures which are a constant around the island. And they are always a beautiful sight. Graceful in their slow death. The stone is always a light faded color. I see so many of them I mistake rocky hilltops for ruined castles. For only a couple of stretches does the land completely flatten out before going back to rolling rocky hills. But even when there are stretches of flat land, hills are never too far and can always be seen in one direction or another.

Rolling hills that stretch for nearly half a mile are perfectly manicured, cultivated and symmetrical on every curve and slope no matter how steep or narrow. The lines are so straight and sharp they resemble marks of a razor made to the line of one's hair on the back of their neck.

At Agrigento the sky was dark— dark blue— and it rained lightly. The police stopped me and the other young person on the train as we walked down the platform towards the station. "Documento." They took down our names and kept us waiting. I was the last to be let go after a plainclothes officer walked around looking at my passport while talking on his cell phone. Then they politely thanked me and I was free.

There was a small prayer room at the end of the platform in the bottom of the station with no one praying. Old men stood around at the counter of the station's café with their macchiatos and cream filled croissants happily doing nothing— saying very little. The young woman behind the counter was unhappy to be there, yet was pleasant to all. The taxi driver that drove me down to the Valley of Temples said his name was Tony Palermo and tried to sell me half a dozen trips to places he was willing to drive me for fifty euros each.

The magnificent temples were somehow still standing— I suspect they must have some modern assistance to keep the whole show going. There were a few other lookers, but the long road connecting the temples was mostly empty and quiet. Lots of piles of oversized rocks that did not make the cut or perhaps had had their day. It was interesting to see how sections of the rocks were carved out like joints for other rocks to slide into, which reminded me of the quarry on Easter Island. It is funny what man does with rocks. Most everywhere rocks are found, some make temples other seek to make themselves from them.

I caught the train just in time after running down the steps to get to the platform. I sat on the other side of the train and enjoyed the landscape of the center of the island once more. I looked at all the farms and vineyards and thought about how all that food, all that earth grows up from this land and lives in all the people here. A perfect and pure cycle, I thought. Again, I thought of how 'of the earth' Italians are, and Sicilians even more so. They are all so calm, unfazed, old souls—they have all lived ten lives. I thought how many Sicilians have a most supreme contentedness about them, a look on their face that seems it would not even be necessary to laugh if they found something amusing. They would laugh and smile somewhere beneath the surface so as not to disrupt their serene and contented disposition. They are the rocks, the trees, the plants, the vegetables, the grapes and the wine.

I spent a few hours at Céfalu, before it got dark. The weather was windy, the sky was black in spots. The clouds fell like streaks of black smoke on to the sea as if a string of fighter pilots had crashed in unison. The sea was four kinds of blue, gradually getting darker as it reaches the horizon. A thrilling rainbow of blue. I hung out at a café next to the Duomo and watched the rain turn to hail which shifted to a brief sunshine before returning to a gray drizzle. All the while having some delicious pistachio and almond cookies drenched in some kind of liqueur.

The train to Messina was moving swiftly when something suddenly gave out and the engine shut off and we were then coasting, slowing down gradually to a halt like a car running out of gas. We sat in a field a mile or two from the coast— there were no lights nearby and occasionally a car would go by on a nearby road. The conductor and ticket man put on orange vests and walked beside the train with flashlights looking underneath. It felt like we were sitting ducks. The inside lights of the train were on and we could be seen from nearly anywhere within half a mile. It seemed a perfect place to rob a train but no bandits graced us with their presence, and after an hour the train was moving again at a slower and somewhat injured pace. Every time it stopped at a station there was a terrible screech. I was happy to arrive in Messina once again. That frontier feel returned to me. There is something about that station that fills me with excitement. Boats and trains and buses going in every direction. I bought a ticket for Rome for tomorrow morning— I would first have to take the boat to Villa San Giovanni at 6:25am. It was now late and only a few stragglers remained in the station along with some homeless men who slept on the benches of the main hall. Puddles of piss collecting beneath them. They mumbled incoherently to one another.

As exciting as the station tended to make me feel, the dreariness of the city was outside and would be menacing perhaps if anyone wanted to hang around and make it so but everybody was elsewhere. I went to the little restaurant across from the hotel where I had been a week ago and I ate a large chicken leg, chips and a Coke.

The hotel was a relief from the wind and rain and made me happy to no longer be stuck on that track in the dark. I managed to read a bit more of D'Annunzio's *Pleasure*. It is so sensually written I can almost taste it.

I am saddened to find out that my beloved home in Bedford is likely to be sold soon. It often feels like the only place I wish to return to. What will I do without that crutch, that place to run away to, as I so often have. I grew up there, I read most of my books there. I love it so much I want to die there, and be buried in the Middle Patent Rural Cemetery. I feel my traveling is only possible because of that place, a place like that is the most perfect thing to circle back and return to. I have known it was inevitable for it to go for a long time but have always been afraid of the day it would go forever. I fear it will be another loss— a hollowing void I will have to fill. I will have to start anew. Why have I spent so much time seeking and looking for so many places to call home, when I have always had one all along? More fool me.

January 17th   Rome

I stood around at what I thought was the spot to get the ferry, but I was wrong. The ticket booth inside the train station where it said ferry tickets were sold never opened and it steadily got closer to the boat's departure. I walked towards the dock and finally found it with a couple dozen people waiting for the boat crew to put the walkway bridges down. There were a few large swells on the short ride in the dark as the land masses of the 'boot' and Sicily glittered all around us. It was like being on a large river. The train went very fast and there was a stop in Naples. Police walked through and checked the papers of some teenagers. Old handguns in white holsters on their sides. Long shiny batons swung from their hips.

The view of the sea was beautiful even at this great speed. The Italians did not think much of it as few looked out the window. Just down at their phones or a book or laptop or straight ahead.

I am happy to be back in Rome, but also feeling there was more to see in Sicily. Another time I suppose. I do not want to be by myself in those small towns or the ghostly towns of Calabria at the moment. It is just too quiet down there. Calabria seems to be getting pushed more and more as a destination, but I do not think it will be spoiled or overrun anytime soon, mostly because it has stiff competition from Amalfi and Sicily— and even Sardinia.

As a matter of fact I saw a picture today in a bookstore of a beach at summertime in Sardinia, and it was so beautiful and colorful I started making plans to visit. A part of me regrets not going there this time around, but the loneliness and solitude of such places is getting to me. I also thought that the one weekly boat from Palermo might get canceled just like the one to Malta.

Sometimes the best place to go is one you know you will love. It does not always have to be an odd or out there place or a new experience. Time and again I have had a similar reaction from people at home or abroad when I tell them I am or have been traveling alone. They usually say, "Really?" "All by yourself? For that long? Just you?" "Why?" I was never surprised and I always understood why they said it. But I have always had my good and bad reasons for traveling alone. I did it for a long time and it began to feel normal and after several trips or journeys with others, good and bad, it was refreshing. So often I would tell them how easy it is. There is no debate over trivial things— no compromising, no putting up with anything or endless discussions of the cost of things. It was just unhinged freedom. But I do begin to feel more as these people do when they question my solitary wandering. It used to seem as though they did not understand traveling by oneself, but now it comes off as me missing out on something. It is not as if I have never traveled with others, I have done quite a lot of that come to think of it. I think some are certainly frightened by the thought of solo travel— not necessarily for all the usual concerns of loneliness and safety, but because of having to deal with all that freedom, having to make decisions and find one's way. They would have to deal with themselves in the process.

I finally bought a coat as it was a little chilly tonight and will be much colder in Tuscany and of course further up in Lombardy. I wanted to avoid the cold, but I want to avoid the small places, too. I want to be around the art, I want to eat all of the paint and canvases.

I was delighted and laughably refreshed to walk into the Anglo-American bookstore this afternoon. It must be a similar feeling a believer gets in a church or an alcoholic at a bar. I browsed longer than anyone and was happily indecisive and picky when it came to choosing some books.

I bought a couple more to go along with the few I have not read yet. I seem to be doing my best to avoid starting Gibbon's *Decline and Fall*. Funny enough, I do feel bad for him after having read a short little biography of Gibbon last year. Somewhat of a sad man— or a man not too blessed in many ways physically or socially. But perhaps gifts of a literary sort are few and far between and Gibbon certainly had those. There is something about all that time he spent in Lucerne. It is a place, unique I suppose, for the English gentleman. There is always talk of Italy and France and even other parts of Switzerland. But Gibbon was faithful to Lucerne. I like that.

I could not read tonight anyway. I am so full of D'Annunzio and doing my best to process much of that pretty book called, *Pleasure*. I keep thinking about it, like it was a conversation I had with a person I once met, and they then ran off into the night. D'Annunzio is a Flaubert; he is the Italian Wilde. I will have to read it two more times. I think more and more critically or rather definitively about reading only the best books. Yes, I stray— but it seems an important thing to do for one's reading life. To read the best. To reread and reread the best or perhaps to reread those that are most touching to you. There is a fear that comes with rereading, though. That the book will not be as good or exciting as it first was or you will see it all differently for the worse. I stop myself from rereading some books because of these fears. Perhaps it is best to reread right away.

January 18th   Rome

I went to the Capitoline Museum and only looked at the two Caravaggio paintings on display in the large center room on the second floor. Every other huge painting had the character of repetitive religious scenes in an old and tired style. Magnificent though they are, I am on a Caravaggio kick. Good paintings never age— they are always boiling with youth— no matter how many times you see them or how long they have been around. The mind behind the eye does not need any context or persuasion to enjoy it. The eye just knows when something is fresh, because great paintings are always fresh. They become like grand traditions and any useful or steadfast tradition never loses its modernity.

It was a pleasant surprise to find there was an Edward Hopper exhibition nearby. At first, I thought he would be out of place in a city like Rome. Hopper is almost overwhelmingly American and therefore a kind of anti-classic painter— but seeing some of those paintings that were all from the Whitney Collection, I remembered just how good he is compared to almost any painter.

His *Soir Bleu* really struck me. It is such a mad crazy painting and does not necessarily seem like something you would expect from Hopper— but it is unmistakably his work— his brushstrokes. It is the work of a man who notices everything. Someone possessing an absolutely playful mind spinning with ideas and deeply aware of what will stimulate his mind and others. Sometimes I think the painting is scary, of course because there is a clown in it and there is always something off about clowns— they are mad, they are crazy – and yet there is always something hilarious and mischievous about them. I often think that many painters no matter how mundane or tame their subjects usually are, have at least a painting or two in them which would display some sort of inner madness or mischievousness. *Soir Bleu* is Hopper's.

I love Hopper, certainly for his paintings, and more specifically for his subjects. The fact that he put so much into illustrating and illuminating architecture as well as landscapes gives me hope for my own paintings. Also, after reading his biography I simply love him because of how he was wholeheartedly an artist for his entire life and never strayed from that path. He was somewhat of an odd guy with an unusually large and monstrous frame for an artist— there was nothing typical or typically artistic in his appearance. He did not dress eccentrically or even act an eccentric— he was rather dull and solitary and looked something like a lawyer. He certainly had a calm patience and measured pace with his work. Nothing wild like Van Gogh. I remember seeing a few pictures of him at his easel and being quite sure that he was painting at a snail's pace. A few well-placed brush strokes per day. It seems only fitting that there was a quote on the wall at the exhibit that said, "the time to take time is in the beginning – at start – to lay out impeccable design so it won't be jostled or skimmed later on." I love that he made his humble but consistent living off of art for so many years and lived in that same little apartment on the top of a brownstone in Washington Square Park until he died. I love that he built that giant easel himself. Looking at so many of his early paintings, the ones on the simplest of subjects in Paris (especially – *Solitary Figure in a Theater*) and even from some scenes in New York— the subject would be something like a staircase or a doorway— it was certainly evident that they were the doings of an amateur— but clearly one with potential— one who is not really missing or lacking talent— but just has not found the subject where his talent would flourish best. A part of me wants to live and work like Hopper. Somewhat of a monkish life. I thought that even before I read his biography, and I thought that while I was reading his biography and of course after, and still. His characters are so often captured in the most interesting kinds of solitary reflection. They are often isolated, lonely or just 'removed' in some way. Those characters are Hopper.

He had no kids, just his wife Jo, an apartment and a house on Cape Cod. He loved movies and literature and those were the things he regularly consumed— his tastes were high but inexpensive— and there is something very satisfying in that combination. High and low. It was nice to see so much of New York and New England in Rome.

Rome was a happy place today. People excitedly swarming around the Spanish steps like bees to a hive. A man making bubbles in the Piazza del Popolo with two sticks and some rope. When a young woman walking towards the man suddenly realized there were bubbles being released into the air, she ran as fast as she could to pop out some of the bubbles. Her high-heeled boots made her quick steps unstable, causing her to miss at first. She looked silly and youthful, but finally was able to squash a small bubble between her palms while standing still. Never have I seen someone older than seven so excited to see bubbles. But they are beautiful little temporary things come to think of it.

I went for a haircut on the via Del Vita and finally I look a little more groomed and hopefully a little more put together. I had steadily been trimming my own hair the past few weeks for I did not want to try to convey how I wanted my hair cut to an old Sicilian barber with no English in one of those small towns. I knew it was best to wait till I got to Rome. A delightful little place, that of course greeted you with an espresso that rivaled any coffee shop in New York. There were more barbers than customers— all in white coats.

Tonight I had a pretty little pasta dish covered in truffles and chestnut sauce.

January 19th   Rome

There was an earthquake yesterday, but I did not feel a thing. Some of the subways and some schools were evacuated. You would have never known. But last night there was an avalanche out in Abruzzo in the mountains and it seems as though the earthquake likely caused it. The avalanche crashed into a nearby hotel and about thirty people died.

January 20th   Florence

It appears there are some survivors of the avalanche in Abruzzo. They miraculously pulled people out of the hotel.

I walked around the Uffizi Gallery for a couple of hours and barely remembered anything from when I was here when I was nineteen. I was eager to get to the end to see the Caravaggio paintings— the Medusa most of all. I had no idea it was on a shield and done as a gift to the Medicis. The snakes of Medusa's head were so realistic I began to wonder just how many times

Caravaggio saw a snake. I loved the richness of the green that surrounded Medusa.

The past sometimes appears boring and its reality is lost in a fog of thought born out of never having experienced it. Thus, so much is considered dull or boringly conservative. But seeing such radical art and things like sculptures of hermaphrodites— it makes me realize that these people from that time and every other time were filled with creative energy, passion and thought. There is nothing stiff about them. They are as wild and eccentric as people today or before them.

I walked up or rather climbed up the four hundred and sixty-three steps to the top of the dome of the Duomo. I was surprised at how unwinded I was. The narrow and winding staircases were a medieval adventure and resembled the bell tower staircases of castles. It was naturally a beautiful view of the city from the top. Difficult to get a sense of the dome itself because I was standing just beneath the very top. Its tremendous height was felt much more from the two balconies inside just below the ceiling's paintings. Up close I was surprised to see the lack of detail or rather the size of the brushstrokes. Painting something that is to be viewed from as far away as the floor is to the ceiling means every stroke is worth much more. But even up close the paintings were still rich and did not lose any of their character. Mad scenes at the lower part of the ceiling were decorated with gruesome monsters in wild sexual acts. Creatures that look like they belong to Bosch. It makes me realize just how small all of Bosch's characters are. For the most part they can fit in your hand. They are less devilish when they are small. So much beauty is because it is in miniature.

It is heaven at the top, with figures painted as if they were sitting in the top of the cupola. I love it when there are figures painted in that position. It is very playful with one's sense of depth perception.

All young people from America, Japan, England and Australia and France were climbing up those narrow staircases. There was a camaraderie amongst us as we all squeezed past one another and climbed in such close proximity to one another. Taking pictures for each other, picking up things that someone dropped and handing them back. Leaning on the walls as groups of girls out of breath stumble and squeeze through taking deep breaths that were pushing hot air out of their red cheeks. Enough light flowed through the small windows to accompany the little lights to make it not feel dank. It was claustrophobic in some places— but the fear of heights could not be realized while climbing as one could never see straight down out of the window. On the way down the lower stairwells were littered in tourist graffiti all near signs that say not to write on the walls. It was a happy climb being surrounded by all those young people. There we all were— straining ourselves as it got more difficult and colder the further we went. All for a glimpse of a different view and in the pursuit of art.

Trump was sworn in today. Few people seem to care in Florence. It almost feels irrelevant which is probably evidence of how over-emphasized the whole election and even the presidency is. It seems to be the only game Americans care about winning anymore. The only thing they wish to talk about. Everyone is putting everything into the person who is in charge, almost as if it were a fetish. Nothing else really matters.

The most that Italians say is that he is some kind of gangster or mafia. He is just a man— don't the Italians know that better than all? Italians usually think in centuries. The age of outrage does not appear to have reached this pretty place. There have been plenty men of power to go through here. Trump is just another man. There will be better and there will be worse.

America from afar looks like the wildest place on earth— a kind of extreme of the human psyche. Perhaps extremely civilized or better yet extremely modern. Modernity squared. There certainly is a lot of life in that country and its people. They are who the world watches.

I went into a number of bookstores today as there are many. The English books are often similar in each and of course the minority overall. I am circling the Medicis— they seem fascinating. I have got my eye on a book called, *Money and Medici*— or is it vice versa?

Either way I am eager to know them. I have a few books to finish now but today I did not want to overload my bag with the Medici books. I could not help myself from buying a little copy of Machiavelli's, *The Prince*. It seemed fitting on this day of power and in the city where he now forever sleeps.

January 21st   Florence

I waited for the bus to Fiesole at San Marco Square with a large group of American girls fresh off an assembly line. They all reacted in group sounds to the little goings-on in front of us— a swarm of pigeons mauling some bread— an old lady just missing the bus. They all talked in a very dull and mediocre way. Funny happenings were responded to with "that's hilarious," and not with laughter. And everything was "literally," this and "literally," that. They made me yearn for and dream of that precious sleep that Sicilians seek.

My only reason for going to Fiesole was to see a place where Frank Lloyd Wright spent a bit of time, I believe, while with a mistress and getting away from his wife and children. That was a hundred years ago.

Fiesole is a little place on a hill. The temperature was below freezing with erratic winds. The temperature struggled to rise even with a prevalent sun, stealing the charm of the square. The colors of everything are made dull by the cold and the green of the surrounding hills is blurred. The people are not interested in much and carry faces that are regretful about getting out of bed. Few are very helpful. I blamed it partially on the cold. The bus drivers do not know what to tell you about a ticket, "I can't do nothing." Neither do the newspaper sellers, nor the cashier at the Tabbachi. They are busy looking down at their phones or something else to help them pass the time.

A bland church sits beside the square and is cold and dark inside. Its large yellow stone is the only color and there is noticeably little effort to beautify the outside as well as the interior. It is a drastic change from the Duomo down in Florence. Two men outside with a large table set up on the curb next to an old dirty white van. A Ducato from the eighties. They talked to one another across the table and in a long pile seemingly dumped out carelessly were all door knockers, doorknobs and several dozen pocketknives.

A cat with the most beautiful coat of fur watched over the Roman amphitheater. Golden stripes sat atop a bed of black while its neck and shoulders were white, and the tail is fat.

There is no sign of Mr. Wright, perhaps I did not dig deep enough, but I just wanted to be there. I find Wright to be anti-European in his style. He is way too modern for Europeans to love him or even admire him the same way they do their artists and architects. He is forever new, forever modern and his style is far too steeped in nature unlike the urban centers of Europe. He is also greatly resemblant of Japanese design. All of these are in conflict with the old-world style of European architecture, the Greek revival, the columns, the stonework. From Fiesole it is evident that Wright is quintessentially and can only be, American.

In the bathroom of the Galleria Academia, tagged on the toilet paper dispenser were the words, "it's a fake!"

David's room is beautiful. Just as I remembered it. The lovely curves above set a soft and sensual mood. The home of a wealthy libertine? The colors are subtle and classy. It is a soft gray stone matching the gray of the curved and straight edged moldings above. The columns are so smooth they look fake and I knock on them to make sure. The circular glass ceiling lets in a calming light not too strong or bright. The floor is a Mediterranean orange accompanied by a sophisticated gray and goes unappreciated or completely missed for everyone is naturally looking upwards.

The female security guards are fierce. One little lady only making it to about five foot two quickly responds to every offense, "No, Signora!" or "No, Signore." Another is one that stays seated mostly, for she is three hundred pounds and her stomach extends passed her breasts. The thighs as thick as the torso of the pretty Russian girl nearby who takes selfies while puckering her glossy gel filled lips. The thighs were so thick it caused her knees to point outward and away from each other. With everything going on above it was a surprise to see the ankle slimmed slightly before reaching her feet which stretched a pair of black leather slip-ons to the brink. They could have been men's shoes. Her calves were weirdly big— grotesque— almost the same size as her head. It is difficult not to take notice of her figure so close to the *David*. And her clothing is so tight and stretched that her body is practically on display, too. Bodies are worthy of display— they can be beautiful and interesting. Enjoyable to observe. Should we not all be naked in this room? It seems appropriate to contemplate ourselves as we contemplate another. The people are so heavily clothed because of the cold weather it is a disappointment when each group arrives so bundled up. There is little to admire as they swish around.

Another of the lady security guards was built like a van and walked like a dimwit— ready to take part in some bureaucratic drivel. The little one barked more and more at the tourists. She wished she had a stick to whack people with. They were a kind of crowd control— museum riot police. Crowds always need reminders— in the form of shepherds. When it gets too loud they aggressively quiet the crowd. They have no grace or charm and are unapologetic. They know they are disliked by the current of people passing through who want to do as they please.

After a while, when the crowd is much smaller and a man with a broom and dust bin sweeps up the floor in the same uninterested way someone would in a school hallway or an airport. He never once looked up.

David's hands and feet dispel the rumors about extremities synchronizing with cock sizes. The right hand seems too large and hangs too low. The hair is an odd style— sensationalized, overblown. It is unrealistic to think someone has hair like that. It is the same shape as Trump's hair but with curls.

I wondered what it must have been like the day a man from Sicily named Piero Cannata attacked the statue with a hammer successfully breaking off the second toe of the left foot before being subdued by guards. He is always described as deranged or crazed. His choice of weapon is somewhat ironic. When asked why he did it, he was quoted as saying, "it was Veronese's *La Bella Nani* who asked me to hit the *David.*" Which sounds like the words of a man who appreciates art or at least takes it seriously. One would think that would be the ultimate prize in art vandalism, but it turns out Cannata went on to be a prolific art vandal. In 2005 he spray-painted a black "X" on a plaque in the pavement of the Piazza della Signora, which commemorates the burning death of Girolamo Savonarola, he did it "because it has a sentence that doesn't make any sense." In 1993 he defaced the fresco by Filippo Lippi in the Prato Cathedral. And also took a knife to the *Adoration of the Shepherds before Baby Jesus* by Michelle di Raffaello Delle Colombe.

In 1999 he scribbled with a marker pen on a Jackson Pollock at the modern art museum in Rome. He had been looking for a work by the Italian abstract artist Piero Manzoni, "but I found an equally ugly one and damaged that instead."

He is not the first vandal of a work by Michelangelo. In 1972, a Hungarian man named Laszlo Toth took a hammer to the piazza at Saint Peter's Basilica disfiguring the face of the Madonna and shattering the left arm. To see such acts of vandalism in such cared for and sensitive places must be a surreal and shocking event. It is a mad kind of expression— but nonetheless still an expression. Some are dissatisfied with things just as much as others enjoy them. And people express themselves differently. It made me think of what Sonny Liston said, "violence is a form of self-expression." Destruction is, too. Those unpleasant ladies are necessary but seem an inadequate force to stop a deranged man like Cannata.

I took a look at the unfinished pieces in the hallway and was reminded of what my friend Armand said about them. "They are mistakes." I did notice a few places that look like they had been chiseled out too much.

David's room was made minimal when stepping into the adjacent salon, Del Ottocento. A wonderfully cluttered room that looks like a private collection.

Only a mad collector would display things in such a manner. It is almost like a working studio where sculptures would dwell. Sculptors have to be madmen, obsessed, certainly more so than painters. To live with the dullness of all that rock for so long, and the dust and the millions of times they have to hear the clicking sounds of rock being chipped and flaked away. It takes a unique soul for such a brutal art.

I slowly strolled around the rectangular room, often pausing to look at the few hundred busts and statues in there that are lifelike enough to inspire reactions one would have towards real people. I was turned off by some, while endeared and seduced by others. The same gossipy thoughts come to mind— his coat is very nice, what a stupid hat, etc.

The men fair far better than the women. A woman's character is more in her color and texture while a man is more defined by his shape. That does not mean the ugliness of some men is not on display. It is plain to see in their balding heads and sagging faces— but each unique characteristic remains.

The pathetic attempts to carve the ladies' hair are sad and dull compared to the beauty and vibrancy of a woman's hair in real life. Men are probably better off in stone; women do much better as living beings. Maybe that is a part of why men so often become gods, idols, myths and legends. Their statues are far more believable and inspiring. A man's ugly bald spot in the flesh looks evidence only of his near decline and fall while a man in stone without hair is a man with a life lived long and full.

The actual girls walking around the rectangular room are prettier than all of the female busts and their skin glows no matter what hue. Even the most boring of the wandering lot has an actual hue and a touch of color to her. The actual men are all uglier. In stone they are full of life and thought, in the flesh they are boring and in the way.

The doglike face of the soprano Virginia de Blasis says nothing of who she is and inspires nothing compared to her neighbor Arnulfo di Cambio whose eyes consist of one lonely stone color and manage to invite you to find something inside him. The veins of his hands flow with dark red blood underneath and his nose is something one would notice from across the room, not for it being ghastly or disproportionate but because it pleasantly sits on his face and tells much of who he is. His face relaxes you and prepares you to listen to him tell some tale. All the ladies in the room have nothing in their faces and almost all resemble one another or look exactly the same which makes one wonder if they actually are the same lady. There is nothing in them that makes you want to love them forever. None of them could be fallen in love with. They do not even inspire a kiss. You cannot imagine any of them doing anything or feeling anything. They look like they smell of stone.

Virginia de Blasis is drowning in stone like she has yet to be chiseled from the mountain. The hands are sadly considered complete by the artist. The face, meant to resemble a woman, is closer to that of a ghost. The book held in the Machiavelli sculpture has more life to it. Though, the face of Bartolini's *Machiavelli* is somewhat done in haste it is saved by the beauty and elegance of the folds and curves of his long robe. Fitting for a man who got dressed in his finest attire for each writing session. The reclining Juno is the only female statue with a little blood flowing through it. It has some inspiring curves and something living in her thighs, but all is lost at the face.

The best sculpture in the whole of the salon has to be that of the majestic old man humbly sitting at the center of the wall of the entrance. It is a delightful homage to Vittorio Fossombroni. This old man in stone is living and hair grows from his ears, the ceremonial clothing that starts at his stomach is swaying as if he were making his way down a corridor. All his wisdom and charm and all the experiences of his years live in his little wrinkled face, and at the hairless peak of his head. You can see that he tied the strings of the robe near his neck himself that morning. You can watch the robe gently sway with his small tired steps. He is just as tired with life as he is with wearing the robe. I wish I knew that man. I wanted to look him up and know what he did and who he really was. So I did. He was an engineer, and economist, a mathematician

The sound of hundreds of teenage girls screaming with excitement quickly rises and becomes deeper resembling a horribly rabid mob as they swarm to the Piazza del Republica to get near the members of an Italian boy band. The two young men stand on the top of the platform of the statue of Neptune. A dozen girls struggle to stay up with them and attempt to take selfies with them. The piazza was once the site of the Roman Forum in the heart of medieval Florence. Around the column hundreds of girls pushing and swarming like bees, screaming and jostling for position. The two skinny young men grin and make playful gestures to the crowd. Those on the top sway and nearly come crashing down, a few do fall, but the masses catch them with help from the growing crowd. Packs of girls approach the square slowly at first but after realizing what is going on one of them would shout directions and then charge into the mass of girls quickly being swallowed up. The Hare Krishnas lead a swaying and dancing procession over the Ponte Vecchio attempting to get the gold sellers and their customers to join them. Florence is a happy and pretty place.

Unfortunately, Italy had some more terrible news today. A bus crash in the north near Verona left sixteen school children dead. They are still searching for survivors in the avalanche. It seems a hopeless proposition.

January 22nd   Florence

This dignified city feels much bigger than it really is for it seems the whole world is passing through.

The Gucci museum is a lovely little sophisticated place that could be the same size of the Uffizi Gallery, but it is subtle, perhaps too subtle, and seems to exist merely to show face in the center of the city. It is a place to gather and not spend too much time staring at exhibits. The café and book room are sophisticated. Wonderfully unique books on Renaissance fashion and all kinds of obscure but beautiful art are stacked on a large table. Funny and provocative titles dotted the books on the table, like Charles Saatchi's, *Be the Worst You Can Be*, which was enticing, but a disappointment for its many comic book blurbs and tired "suitable for those who are new to reading or thinking."

Florence becomes suddenly dizzy and not just on the timeframe of rush hour. Crowds appear and detours have to be made accordingly in order to get anywhere. These crowds are loud, like a buzzing mass of hornets.

Across the square in front of Basilica Santa Maria Novella at magic hour, some birds fly in a large beautiful pack. Suddenly nature appears in an urban place. They make the fastest and most beautiful turns, they are an irresistible sight, a rollercoaster without a track. They must be, because their flight path makes no sense. We followed each other, for I went to the station to check some train times and they ended up out front in a frenzy popping in and out of the trees. The intense sound of birds reminded me of the sound of the girls yesterday swarming around those two boys.

I cannot help but notice the extravagantly dressed ladies you see idling together or leisurely reading a paper in a café. The outfit usually consists of oversized furs that cost more than cars, a few large jewels, a sophisticated hat— often a puffy beret, and two-inch heels. Their looks are gone but they look content in knowing how rich and fabulous they are.

I thought I was in my room for the night when I split my pants as soon as I got back to my room. So I went down to the H&M to get a new pair. When I looked up where it was I noticed the reviews and each one of them said it was a good store, but they all complained about how they could no longer go there because it always smelled so terribly. I knew it was near the old market but there was no food sold there anymore, so when I got there I was still surprised to find that there was a rotten egg smell throughout the store and even though the store was busy you could see people holding their noses or covering their faces with something. I even heard a few people say, "I cannot take the smell anymore, I have to leave."

Rome and Florence certainly have revived me after a week. Sicily and even Calabria seem so many centuries away— so old and getting older faster than most places. Time goes the opposite way. They are not impressed by modernity.

January 23rd   Florence

The towns seen along the ride towards Lucca were not particularly pleasing to the eye. The abandoned stone houses in the fields were more charming. The train was a filmstrip quickly moving along, and the towns are a sad audience— looking back at life, standing still— those poor villages burdened by the regular passing of noisy trains. It was a relief whenever nature returned. Rows of narrow white trees and some vineyards were a welcomed sight.

At the station in Lucca you are confronted with an endless wall with millions of bricks, almost too large for the city behind it. From the station it looks impossible to get into the city but at its opening kids walked through the small narrow stairwell whose walls are covered in pathetic graffiti that could only be done by drunken amateurs.

Lucca's charming and intimate piazza just beyond the wall had barely a soul passing through. The freezing cold cathedral had a residue of incense that lingered in the frigid air. Its best feature being at the side, Il Voltes Santo, with its dark-skinned Christ in a black robe and insane eyes. The altar disrupts the flow of the cathedral but is a pleasant detour. A cross hanging over the center of the aisle appears as an odd accent at first but starts to float when walking beneath it and the chain from which it hangs cannot be seen. Anything that floats is amusing. The playful columns of the façade and the sound of the nearby fountain remind one of Venice. The color, though it is far too singular and its few strips of black stone a lazy attempt to improve its style. It really could be something much better, perhaps if it was given the same green as the Duomo of Florence.

I spent no more than fifteen seconds at the church in the Piazza San Michele, before rushing off to Pisa. Lucca was dull and a middling kind of place. Too big to charm, too small to inspire.

It was a much prettier ride from Lucca to Pisa. Well placed hills with interesting curves. Much more groomed and cultivated land, flattening out entirely after San Giuliano Terme.

I got off the train at Pisa San Rossore and was much closer to the tower than I would have been at the Centrale Stazione. Therefore, I saw the tower before the city itself. The tower and the whole little complex are a wonderfully weird sight. Weird and intriguing enough to make you wait for years to watch it fall. My smile never left me the entire time, for I found the whole thing to be incredibly funny. It was a constant joke being played, a kind of charade or something out of a nether world. The funniest of follies.

Up close one realizes how massive it is and indeed how beautiful. Perhaps there is no bell tower more beautiful in the world. Its steps are made even smoother, like a thick animal skin, and wavy from the millions of visitors. There is something romantic about worn down steps. It is absolutely joyful to be at the top of the tower for the view of the cathedral and the surrounding countryside. But just to be atop the tower was something to love in and of itself. Everyone was excited to be there. There are more Japanese people there than I have ever seen anywhere outside of Japan. It would make you think that there are more Japanese than Italians in Pisa. And of course the Italians are thoroughly bored by everything going on. They want nothing to do with the tourists or the monuments.

Inside the cathedral, workers hammered loudly at the top of a scaffold. The ceiling is far too grandiose for the rest of the cathedral. It was more enjoyable to look back at the light coming through the windows over the entrance than it is to look at the altar. The pulpit standing out much like the ceiling.

The baptistery is a beautifully shaped and decorated building from the outside, but inside it becomes a thoroughly hollow and odd place making one not want to have their child baptized there. Far too much work has been done for it to be considered a folly. Void of any accent or decoration it appears more fitting for a secret society and their *Eyes Wide Shut* parties rather than a religious ceremony.

One cannot help but take note of the well-manicured grass. It is sophisticated and mature, the lack of gardening removes any chances of pretentiousness. No sense in trying to drown out the beautiful structures with plants and bushes.

Of all the buildings in the little complex, the Camposanto is the most magnificent and actually 'human' building. Still a showpiece like all the rest, yet it is far more homely and inviting than all the others, and is a magnificent kind of cemetery. Birds fly down the hallways like they are on a racetrack. The sudden changes of movement shifts the light of the building in wonderful ways creating other dimensions with the shadows coming in through the columns and stonework. One side covered in sun, the other dim and much more cool. I was saddened to find out that the *Triumph of Death* fresco was not on display that day. But there were other intriguing frescoes on the walls. I studied a large one near the entrance with the monsters looking back at me, while the pigeons hooted compulsively from the beams of the ceiling. Some particularly ghastly scenes were depicted. A woman having her tongue pulled out, a stick going through a man's ass, out his mouth and into another man's mouth, spinning like a rotisserie chicken. Snakes were all over the place. I did a few laps around before making my way to the river.

The houses and buildings along the Arno are a splendid sight, making one realize that Pisa is a grand city in its own way. The width of the sky over the river opens the entire city making it seem larger. A man leisurely rides his bike along the river while his fat golden dachshunds run devotedly alongside without a leash.

I smiled the whole time I walked along the river and was incredibly filled with joy going over the bridge to the side without any sun. I thought of all the things I had seen and how nice it has been bathing in all of this luxurious beauty.

Italy is a pleasure bath for your eyes. You never use them more than you do in Italy. You are constantly looking in every direction for there is always something to look at, and so often it requires looking upwards. Where else does one look up at something beautiful as much as in Italy? All the senses align and filter through the eyes. So many pleasurable sights make the eyes activate all the other senses in the other direction. It is food and music and sex for your eyes. It is an incredibly fulfilling feeling to see so much beauty.

I have been reading some of Henry James's *Italian Hours* on the last few train rides and in my room at night. I wish I had started it a while ago and used it as a primer before arriving in Italy. I have jumped to the chapters focused on Tuscany and it is a double pleasure to read about Tuscany in words by the master while being here. The Rome and Venice chapters look enticing and perhaps I should save them for when I am actually there.

Reading is such a pleasure. I do not think I could be without it. I am starting to think the same of Italy. James said, "Pisa may be an adult place to live in, but it's an ideal place to wait for death." One could say the same for the whole of Italy.

January 24th   Siena

I was gloomy this morning for I gaze too often at the faces of others. The absence of morning smiles brings me down, so I stopped looking. Thankfully, I was somewhat cheered by a delicious cup of chocolate at Gilli. You see the same men working early in the morning that you do late at night. Of course, I am sure they sleep there in suit and tie.

The sound of Florence's train station was lyrical to me. The robotic male voice over the loudspeaker followed by a more breathy and lighter female voice oddly gave me pleasure. The sound of travel. There are hordes of people. Florence feels like the busiest of crossroads.

On the train the young man across from me took from his paper bag a book that was somewhere around fifteen hundred pages thick and started reading from the beginning, moving his finger with each sentence along the pages as he read.

By the time we got to Certaldo, the whole car and much of the rest of the train had emptied out and the landscape became more natural and covered in trees whose leaves were long gone. The train car warmed as the sun filled the seats from the east above the low, tree covered hills.

Soon enough I was in Siena's delightful square which pleases just about every part of one's mind and being. People lay down in the sun sloping downwards towards the tower. Some completely flat on their back looking straight up and in a deep sleep. Others sat staring towards the tower, but they look to be staring out to an endless ocean. I did the same. Italians soak in the sun, chatting, sleeping—taking the casual bite of a Panino. The tourists agonize over the perfect pose for a photo. Only a hideous soul with a black heart could not enjoy lounging in Siena's square. There is a contentment in accomplishing absolutely nothing. Though, I suppose it is much quieter than summer, this winter season is not without bustle and activity. Around the square is a slow-moving pedestrian highway, alert dogs wandering, and hunched over old ladies somehow still walking— miraculously made it down to the square from the rest of Siena's sloping streets.

Waiters throw out small bowls of uneaten potato chips onto the edge of the square for the pigeons. Their necks glitter in the sun and at a closer look they are pretty except for their feet. Some of which are missing. Those with one leg idle while those still intact move at a much more active pace. A few pigeons attempt a leisurely pace down the slope of the square but begin to slide on the slippery slope, before bailing out.

I sat in one of the cafés overlooking the square and a Chinese couple sat at the next table. Very much the tourist or honeymoon type and without any Italian or English communication with the waiters it quickly became a unique experience. The waiters prepared the table and soon enough, two glasses of red wine had arrived and they were free to soak in all of the beauty of the city and the country before them. After a minute or two I watched them spoon clumps of grated Parmesan cheese into their glasses of red wine, clink them together and continue to drink at a leisurely pace with a certain look of satisfaction in having partaken in Italian culture.

It is easy to notice that the beloved Palio is not taking place. Just like being on the field of an empty baseball stadium. One expects to see horses in Siena's streets for this city is a castle. One expects the near constant clicking of horseshoes on those hard stones gradually smoothing them out. Except it is the hollow and weak pitter patter of rubber soled shoes. The sounds of horses' hooves in the city would provide a melodic echoing off the walls, somewhat frightening but also enchanting when a horse's trot takes shape and gains rhythm. At night the city becomes more of a castle, with long streets looking like oversized hallways or the walkways on the top of the wall. Siena proves that there are many beautiful colors of brick and no other kind of stone or even paint is necessary to make a beautiful city. Even with all the obvious new and fresh look of the retail shops, Siena is nowhere near modern. It looks perfectly unchanged, untouched.

The quiet and lonelier streets are dim and hilly and look all kinds of suspicious. I feel as though I am naked and vulnerable without carrying some sort of dagger or some other medieval weapon in my belt. But such fears really are one's own fantasies, for there is little danger to be found and no need for a dagger other than for opening an envelope.

January 25th   Siena

A big cup of chocolate at Café Fiorella this morning brightened and woke me up.

There were some nicely painted old book covers on display amidst the endless shelves of Siena's city records at the Museo delle Tavolette di Biccherna. If only all books were considered with such care and style. The lady who followed me around the entire time let me out onto the balcony for the tremendous view of the square. It is an ever-changing work of art evolving throughout the day from the changes in light and the masses of people lounging, idling and passing through.

I stepped into a classy place with high prices in search for something to lunch on other than pizza or spaghetti carbonara. I asked for a steak and the waitress warned me of how big it was— and I said, "it's ok, it's ok." They then brought it out raw on a silver tray to show me and it was indeed a large porterhouse, nearly a kilogram. When cooked it was as rare as could be, fat at all and not on the bone. I took note of the few other patrons taking note of me. It was then a leisurely stroll through the hearthstone streets back to the sunny square where I leaned up against one of the stone pillars and took a small siesta along with my fellow humans. An absolutely enjoyable place to read, take notes, listen to Sam Cooke, lounge around, watch the people, contemplate the Torre del Mangia piercing the sky— and be warmed by the slowly shifting sun. This is an afternoon in Tuscany. The faces of the patrons at the tables of Bar Il Palio turn red in the sun as they sip the ice filled wine glasses and hold their small dogs tightly to their chest.

January 26th   Siena

Even without walking up and down the steep streets it was a sleepy day. It is only right to not try to do much other than let Siena soak into your skin. The streets were more than enough. I stumbled upon some churches but did not wish to take much note of their details or character or even their charm. I was much more enchanted by the winding streets that slope upwards and downwards and curve and straighten out as they please. A river of stone on which you can easily glide around for hours, which almost always leads to the square where you find yourself laying in the sun.

I had another Florentine steak this time flavored with five different kinds of pepper. Green, red, black, white and a Chinese pepper. A bite was accompanied by a burst of floral fragrance. It was like biting into flowers. The restaurant was started by a former Palio jockey and decorated with all kinds of Palio memorabilia including many colorful jockey helmets.

January 27th   Florence

Soft winter fields of a yellowish brown and the crooked branches of bare trees line the root up to San Gimignano. The scene of an ancient castle covering an entire hilltop gives one much to ponder.

In the Piazza della Cisterna a lady struggled to set up a ladder at a gelato shop below a large sign proclaiming, "The Best Ice Cream in the World."

The staple picture of every Italian village is a small group of elderly men in the piazza's sunniest spot talking boisterously and trying to make each other laugh. San Gimignano's was no different. A man inside the church policed the tourists— 'No photo! No capello!' The frescoes were beautiful in the cold dark church that is the heart of the little square. Almost every building is of the same color stone the only difference being the size and of course the height of the towers. It still makes the town an organic place to have grown from the hill it sits upon. The towers are kind of like trees. Most little shops sell tourist kitsch and idling villagers are bored of the foreigners and their predictable ways. I wondered if the younger villagers have known any different. The hordes of travelers passing through year after year is a kind of tradition. In summer, I can only imagine the crowds would gridlock the town so much as to steal its quaint charm.

I found a quiet little salumeria selling all kinds of local cheeses and meats covering every inch of the shop. I bought the most delicious little brick of cheese, that tasted like a glass of cream. It was earthy, too, and I imagined it was mixed with specks of dirt from the hills around the town. This was how I imagined those Tuscan hills tasted. I walked back to the piazza with my cheese and sat in the now much larger sunny spot that the now much larger group of old men still occupied. They talked louder and laughed more, clearly making fun of each other. I looked across the square and saw the sign for the world's best ice cream had disappeared. I innocently thought it was no longer the best. I enjoyed the raspy voices of the old men's laughter and I enjoyed a little piece of cheese. I imagined it was the only kind of cheese those old men and in *Il Cavadenti* it is easy to miss the small child at the front left covered by shade.

I was surprised to find myself enjoying the *Sleeping Cupid* as paintings of children always seem a bit creepy. The artist spending so much time staring at a child model...but there was something more to this portrait of Cupid, something much greater and beautiful. The darkness at the top of the small painting created all kinds of emotions. When I spoke to one of the ladies attending to a nearby room, she told me of how it is believed that Caravaggio painted the *Sleeping Cupid* from a recently dead child.

Once I found the Caravaggio paintings, they were all I wanted to look at. But they were not the only thing to see. There was a particularly nice little room at the end of a hallway called the oval room which we were only allowed to peek into from the doorway. Some ceilings are so rich and thickly covered in gold it makes the Mediterranean orange and white of the floor look like a mud room for a seaside home.

You look up so much not only straining your neck, but your back, too. A place like Pitti is not made for walking through trying to take everything in at once. It thoroughly discombobulates you and forces your mind to see it all at once as one large painting. There really is a great emphasis on painting for much of the wall decoration is painted to appear as intricate molding. They are so realistic you find yourself getting as close as possible to see if it really is a painting or not.

Then other things start to look painted in the third dimension are an illusion. I was nearly ten feet from a column before it revealed itself to my eyes to actually be painted onto the wall. There is a deep love of painting at Pitti. These palaces really are the coldest of places. Much of the design and art can only truly be enjoyed from laying on a bed or chaise over months or years. They are so beautiful but yet so large they could not possibly make one truly feel at home unless you were a pure megalomaniac.

Some paintings are so large and complex and surrounded by other equally complex paintings that you resign yourself to the simple ornate pleasure of the few patterns of the red covering an empty wall space. I began to take note of the intense jumbling of paintings.

In one room a large painting had been removed and only its gold frame remained. The blank and darkened pink wall space stands out, somewhat of an eyesore but also funny and mischievous— an art in and of itself. For a moment one thinks the painting was stolen. But also one thinks of what the painting was. I probably would not have noticed it had it been there among the clutter of all the other paintings. Perhaps its absence was more forceful than its presence. Sometimes a painting should have its own room.

The Boboli Gardens were there and much of its color absent on this wintery day. Though, it was still a lovely place to stroll for much of the green in the grass remains along with the leaves of Cypress trees. The manicured grass and walkways provide an orderly landscape and remind those strolling that there is a palace behind this garden. A good garden like Boboli remains beautiful even without the colors and flowers of a blooming spring and prosperous summer.

January 29th   Florence

More families and revelers filled the piazzas on this sunny Sunday than yesterday. Florence is met with waves of people that rise and retreat on any given day.

Along the river, people sat atop the walls and remove their jackets to enjoy the spring like temperatures. I walked past the heavily guarded US Consulate building that sat beside the river to the shabby park over the next bridge. Though the green was pleasing the park seems evidence of Florence being a much smaller place and not so grand. At one point, Florence starts to become an urban sprawl lacking much charm, which is from the Ponte San Niccolo to the Ponte della Vittoria— and that is quite a lot— but one still hopes Florence would stretch for miles and miles more.

January 30th   Florence

It was very cold in Borgo San Lorenzo this morning. They are not accustomed to visitors this time of year— some looks of surprise and maybe suspicion. Most are at the few small cafés for they are the only thing open. It is always men gathering. Women are rarely seen in the street or cafés— if they are in the street, they are hustling off someplace. I came back early but waited a while at the station for the next train and watched the surrounding hills become more colorful as the sun struggled with the clouds. The apartment block set next to the station and its residents slowly came out one or two at a time. Not everyone was Italian, people from Asia and Africa. It surprised me and I realized those small towns are not as small as they appear to be. Quite often you find that in an Italian village there are people from all over the world.

January 31st   Florence

Florentine cuisine is not as overtly on display as in other parts of Italy. The art is on display and everything is geared toward that while in the south, in Sicily and Naples, food is everywhere, and the art is at the top of a mountain. Florentines are much more reserved or guarded perhaps than in other towns and cities. It is almost as if they are all plain clothed soldiers.

It is not the same as Sicilians— it's not about what they are— it's about what they stand for— and that is— all of Florence.

I took a walk across the river and up the hill to Piazzale Michelangelo. Even with the overcast sky it was a charming view. It is always there— like a painting—changing but still mostly all there all the time. A view like that of the city of Florence stays with you the same way a painting in the Uffizi does. How long can one stare at the best views and the best paintings and sculptures. Forever, I quickly concluded. There is, of course pleasure brought to it from the anticipation of seeing each image. It is not just a view or a painting— it is the walk up the hill or the search in the museum. One eventually looks away from the prettiest of images and maybe goes back to them. Then there is remembering those images, places, and paintings. And then there is forgetting. Perhaps, that is the real mark of any image, view, or painting— it is never forgotten even after many years have passed. I wonder how much if not all or none of Michelangelo's works were created with the thought of not being forgotten. It was something easy to think about this morning when I stood in the Medici chapel. I do not know much about any of the Medici other than they were ruthless political actors. All their enemies and victims and the pain inflicted upon seem to be forgotten in a way, it cannot be felt, only imagined. But the Medici are not— and that must be the ultimate on this cold wet Wednesday at mid-morning. They filled the pews of the side chapel inside. Before the small gates to the chapel was a table on which each person signed their name into an elegantly thin folding notebook with only a few pages. Beside it was a little sign that read, "In Memoria di Gianfranco Pernici."

About a hundred people greeted each other like a family. They generally were older but there were a dozen or so young blonde women. Many of the old men sported the same hairstyle— gray around the back and sides and a tanned and shiny bald spot at the top. Many of the older ladies shared a similarly short maroon colored hair— one with an unfortunately thin spot.

I sat in a chair behind the gate and looked through as they awaited the priest's arrival. A bell rang— everyone stood and a bald priest in a baggy purple robe began to speak. From his steady old voice came the clearest and most majestic Italian. Each word clearer than the next. It was the sound of a calm man who had never once raised his voice his entire life. When he repeatedly said, 'Hallelujah,' the syllables were beautifully stretched out creating the most soothing sound. And the worshipers tried to match him, but collectively they were a muffled background noise. The service was not somber— and everyone was stoic and dressed casually.

The casket was put into a curvaceous Mercedes hearse and followed the priest who walked slowly around the Parco il Prato towards the Cimiterio di Fraternita—all at the service followed behind a hearse and they could not be seen after a few minutes.

I was left beside the Parco il Prato, which is Arezzo's loveliest little space, resembling a small private cricket field— circled by trees and a gravel cross of a walkway in the center stretching to each end. To the north there is a valley crowded with houses and some hills. I went the other way down the hill through the city to catch the train.

I did not wake up today for I never went to sleep. I was rattled with insomnia all last night. I watched midnight arrive and January turn to February which meant I had left two months ago. Yesterday and all through that sleepless night I was riddled with loneliness. I have put myself in a kind of cage, which I have the key to, but I won't let myself out. I am stubborn and stop myself time and again. I am pulled by the comfort of home in New York on one hand and seeing more of Italy on the other. And both of these forces only seem to be swimming in the same solitary well.

I thought of what my friend Armand once said to me, "It does not matter where you are, just do something so that people will come to you no matter where they are."

February 3rd   Perugia

The streets are just as quiet and empty as Siena. Perugia also looks like a castle, but one built over a longer period of time, whereas Siena looks more planned and built all at once. The Piazza IV Novembre is Perugia's natural crossroads fit with the peculiar and circular Fontana Maggiore. Surrounded by an iron fence and just too hard to see into its lowest pool— it is more suited to a private estate than a public square.

There is little shame in the clustering of rocks that shape the exterior of the Cattedrale di San Lorenzo which looks like the geological version of shabby chic as do a number of Perugia's other churches. Like Siena, there is stone all over the place, reinforcing the castle look and with the tall buildings that border the piazza it also gives one the sense of a city at the bottom of a quarry.

Coming up the hill from the train station leaves one confused and discombobulated, thinking the ride much longer than it is. The center of the town is perhaps the most well-fortified town in all of Italy. You wind through much of the suburban sprawl that falls down the hill from the center which sits on top often with the flatness of a landing pad. In more than a few places you can stand beside the granite railing overlooking the rows of dark green hills of Umbria. At these edges you get a sense of just how high up Perugia is. But the sense of that height does not leave one while heading towards the piazza for the strong winds often accompany you. Now, once one finally makes it inside the Cattedrale di San Lorenzo you truly and suddenly feel you are at Perugia's peak for you are confronted with the same sudden silence a hiker is confronted with when reaching the top of a mountain. It was not a silence to be described as deafening for it was much more peaceful and the ears remain alert and searching. It is also not to be described as eerie or anything of the sort, for it was much fresher and more alive, therefore putting one under a sort of dreamy illusion. The height of the ceiling was abnormally high and gave off the same vertigo one gets at a mountaintop. Not just from looking down, but up, too. Just as shifting clouds can play with the sense of perspective. The ceiling was a kind of sky. And most of the beauty of its interior is in the ceiling, but as dark as it is it takes some long straining glances to let your eyes fully soak it all in. When there is a sound made from someone coughing or whispering it lingers in the form of a long dull echo. At Cattedrale di San Lorenzo, never have I seen more carvings of skulls and bones than I have in all of Italy's churches. Italians appear as comfortable with death as they do with life, so they encompass and embrace it in their churches, too.

The dark greens in the rooms are what one expects of a city surrounded by lush greenery and isolation. They are the colors of a New England boarding school— somewhere with "academy" in the name— and a classical school mascot—Spartans or Trojans.

Just before the western walls of the city, sits a nearly forgotten church, with a grassy square in front, known as the Piazza San Francesco. It was a structure with almost three churches connected to each other. One much like the main cathedral, blocky and stoned white. The middle one nearly unnoticeable and the little one facing the grassy piazza, known as the Oratorio di San Bernardino. It had the most dazzling pink and mint green facade and looked more out place than any church I have ever seen. It was as if someone personally commissioned it from being tired of all the white stone of the other churches. It could have been in Rome or by the sea or something a bored Marie-Antoinette would have wanted disassembled and moved to her corner of Versailles. Inside, it was nearly blank save for the bricks that wrapped around the curved ceiling. But the minimal interior did not detract from the magnificence of its facade.

Beside via Priori there is a charming and narrow street called via Steffano that winds less than it slopes down to a little piazza with a quirky church. From the piazza it looks suspicious but young students suddenly march out of it and the street begins to brighten. Walking up it you are greeted by a wall draped in ivy, while cold and damp stone gives a sense that there was once a stream or creek running down and emptying into the piazza.

There is no event too large or grand for the Piazza IV Novembre. It is a square that appears to have witnessed countless military parades and thousands of public executions.

February 4th   Perugia

At Assisi, I approached the Basilica San Francesca and was greeted by its harmonious bells sounding off for a few minutes.

The colorful interior of the church's ground floor removed the whitewashed exterior from my mind and I was immediately taken by the intricately tiled arches, the seductive blue of the ceiling and the painted walls. The ceiling is an odd height for the church, even though the main church is directly above and appears to hang downwards. An uninspiring place for a church, almost cave-like. But the frescoes make you forget about dimensions and proportions. The colors are brilliant and the dark scenes entertaining. One of a man standing beside a skeleton.

On the lowest level is Francis' humble tomb in the center of a cross shaped chapel. A cave within a cave, and very well lit. A dozen people were in deep concentrated prayer. There is no color down below, only stone and some iron gates on each side of the tomb. No tourist lingers for there was nothing to look at. Only those that prayed and me.

Much of the same design of the ground floor church continues in the much larger upper Basilica. Only the ceiling is much higher and more suited to a cathedral. The colors have much more room to breathe and at times blend together. The ceiling is a robe of color flowing in the wind.

I took all the steps and slopes up to the wonderfully named Rocca Maggiore to look out over the valley. The sky was endlessly covered in whitish gray clouds. Not a speck of blue or light getting through. It was another tower climbed. I must go up all the towers. After all, they are there. It is worth the sweat and struggle.

Naturally, I found a humble salumeria and sat on a bench with the meats and cheeses and fed some pigeons. Then I spent thirty euros on deliciously high-end pastries at a little bakery on my way back down the hill.

I took the bus back and seeing Assisi get smaller was just as charming as watching it grow as I had approached this morning. The bus wound through muddy little towns and I wondered what could make a beautiful and mystical town like Assisi even more beautiful. I suppose, to believe in God. But that did not happen today.

February 5th   Bologna

A city like Siena or Perugia is just as natural as any mountain or cliff or river, evidence that modernity is just as natural— just as continental plates can shift so can the foundation of any castle or institution or city. Something built a thousand years before that still stands is not only testament to the ingenuity of man but begs the question— had it been built two thousand years before could it still be here? Still growing another branch like a tree? Perugia is older than many rivers and trees and rock formations. Why not consider it a natural being or a part of nature?

I left early this morning and walked down the hill winding through the streets— the city all to myself— the only company was a black cat yet to cross my path giving a suspicious stare. Halfway down I gazed back up and realized there was no going back up from that point because it would take three times as long. Once you are that far down, the city shuns you. It tells you to keep going because you decided to leave in the first place.

Hidden in the hills is a network of stairs— old, new and ancient within a few sloping streets that make a pathway, albeit maze-like, from the top of the city down to the train station.

I did my best to get to Cortona on this wet Sunday. At Camucia, there was no sign of a bus or taxi and I did not want to unsettle one of the locals by asking for a ride. I gave up and walked back to the little station. Cortona was covered in fog and my socks were wet. Cortona will have to be for another day.

Porticos, porticos, porticos, and more porticos. That is what Bologna is. Covered in porticos. The city is red all over— dipped in red— and the porticos are everywhere and there may be more porticos here than anywhere else in the world. They are not decorated homogeneously for there are many different designs and murals or one solid color decorating the curved ceilings and floors of the porticos. They shield you from the rain and if the sun were out it would shield you from that, too. They line nearly every street on each side, and the streets without porticos are quickly a disappointment and one momentarily leaves the city of Bologna whenever not sheltered by a portico. All of these covered walkways turn Bologna into a palace. If Siena and Perugia are castles, then Bologna must be a palace. It is a fitting description for a city that on the surface is so unequivocally rich and well-off.

The students around the university drank in jolly packs, their legs dangling off the raised sidewalks beneath badly lit porticos. Most either have significant facial hair or a big mop of it on their head. They look just like radical students should. The area around the university, though still beautiful— is dirtier and at times in need of repair. Political graffiti is on nearly every wall.

A prominent Mural to Francesco Lorusso— a far left activist allegedly killed by police in the nineteen seventies and now a martyr of sorts who bears a resemblance to Fidel Castro. Another mural with a female Kurdish soldier and the words, 'Kobane Resiste,' in support of the Kurdish town in northern Syria that was under siege from ISIS. All the students look like the typical traitors to their own class— there is no working-class condition on the surface to be seen in Bologna. It only appears that the oldest university is made to look shabbier than it really is in the hope of appearing rebellious. Rebellious for the sake of it. Rebellious as a style. Rebellious out of boredom. These sorts of movements and beliefs always buzz over the most well-off cities like flies over a hippo or fish beside a whale. Their demands fade and others start to demand things of them, for once.

February 6th   Bologna

From the start it was a day meant for staying in bed, but I gave way to my desire to wander. The weather was an unavoidable nuisance and did a great deal to tire me out. The rain made the cold even colder and there was not a hint of sunlight. There was the anticipation of snow at every moment. Without all the city's red color I would have thought I was in London. The porticos became a kind of refuge and I found myself pausing inside to collect myself after being caught in the rain-soaked piazza. The pleasantly odd spectacle of Bologna's two leaning towers sat stoically— enduring the elements in the Piazza di Porta Ravegnana. I paid the three euros to the fat man in a little booth a few steps up the Torre degli Asinelli and then took all the steps to the top. It got colder and my hands became numb from the handrails of the wooden staircase which were chillier than they looked. The ugly interior was dungeon like— a dungeon in the sky that narrowed as the top neared. From the street level it is easy to appreciate the beauty of Bologna— from the top of the thousand-year-old tower one's eyes get to swim in the sight of the red roofs and yellowish walls that clutter together in one colorful view. Bologna is even more charming all at once just as it is street by street and portico by portico.

By the time I sat for lunch at Buca Manconi I was tired and my eyes were telling me to sleep. But I indulged on Lasagna Verdi and Cotoletta alla Bolognese— which was a thin piece of veal covered in Parma ham and then covered in cream.

I spent much of the afternoon resting my cold and sore legs and began reading *The Charterhouse of Parma*.

Tonight, I again wandered around the university and looked at the graffiti. There were some groups of students collected around a table under a portico having a quiet poetry reading. The rain had stopped and it was warmer. The streets were quiet.

February 7th   Rimini

I missed the fast train so had to settle for the local, but all that meant was the train sat for extended periods at each station, not more stops. The faces of the people on the train were decidedly different. They did not have a stereotypical Italian look to them as was more prevalent in Bologna. Everyone was some kind of unique mixture— and there were more than a few young men with orange or red hair and pale skin. When I arrived in Rimini the feeling in the air of being in a decidedly different place was palpable. It was like crossing from Italy to Ireland or Russia.

In fact, I had thought just that as the landscape was flattening out along the tracks and the clouds slowly evaporated into the blue sky. The sunshine was pleasant over the cultivated fields. Though, there was nothing glamorous about this landscape— it was a place of work— and looked like an Italian Poland or Italian Crimea— the air still cool meant summer in Siberia.

If the approach and the first glance of Rimini does not solidify its resemblance to Eastern Europe, a short walk through the city does. If everything was not closed the city would not look so sad and perhaps more well-off, chances are there is more to Rimini in the summer and in the heat. All the buildings are small— never more than four stories. You quickly find yourself saying how does anyone make a living around here? What do people do here?

Restauranteurs work busily even though they only have one or two customers—some have none. Each restaurant looks like someone tried to convert a room of their house into a business— quirkily decorated with colors that don't match and flooded with random knickknacks.

If Rimini's beach were not so grand in length and width the city would be hopeless. But the beach looks ready to accommodate the summer wishes of a million people. Perhaps after seeing a beach town like Positano one can never see any other in quite the same way or with reasonable expectations. Rimini's beach takes on the look of a place that is more functional than charming. Perhaps that is why it seems like it could be set alongside the Black Sea or maybe even the Caspian Sea. It is indeed a place where Russians and Ukrainians come to vacation— it is Italy but it is also cheap. There are even signs and menus in Russian, too. I walked along the shore— crushing the white soft clamshells under my feet. Some trash washed up and was left to idle in the lazy tide. There were many soles of shoes for some reason. The Soviet feeling only furthered by the thunderous presence of military helicopters racing back-and-forth above the shoreline.

February 8th   Ravenna

It is a pleasure to no longer be lingering in Rimini or San Marino. A nauseatingly slow and winding bus ride went through an oddly modern landscape of car dealerships, office parks, industrial sites and to top it off an airplane graveyard, just before crossing into San Marino. The little place is a quirky hill that only seems stubborn for wanting to remain an independent country. Italy must have been too uninterested to do the work of integrating or invading it. One wonders why there are not more little places of stubborn people seeking sovereignty. There were a number of gun shops on a few streets with an overwhelming supply. When I asked one of the sellers about it he revealed to me that they were all air guns. And some recent regulation in Italy was an opportunity for him, "so we created a market." I did not linger, for the short amount of time I was there already felt as if I had spent too long.

I was happy to arrive in Ravenna and find myself nibbling on a Piadina with Squacquerone cheese. I managed to step into the Basilica Sant Apollinaire Nuovo before it was dark outside and did my best to soak in the mosaics. All the gold is above the portico arches and never reaches ostentation even though there is clearly an abundance of it. The white robes of the Martyrs of the Virgins are a distraction. Each side is best viewed from under the opposite portico. There was not enough time to spend with them— for it would take days to fully see and appreciate them, perhaps longer. It was dark before I could get to any of the other churches. I returned to reread some of Henry James' Ravenna essay— and I took heart to what he wrote of his own visit to the Sant Appollinaire. He referred to the Martyrs as saints— and I suppose they are both. He referred to them as possessing an odd, knowing, sidelong look, yet at the same time carried a kind of sweetness.

It was dusk and for a few minutes I was alone in the church and I could feel the stares of the saints looking down at me— they were mature and indeed all-knowing in their expressions. I did indeed have the urge to sit, to remain— but not to pray.

February 9th   Ravenna

The dome of the Basilica San Vitale is almost impossible to fully appreciate without laying on the floor to stare directly upwards. It is as if it is not meant to be completely seen at once by someone who has the church all to their self.

The soft greens of the altar are pleasant to stare at and easy on the eyes. On the altar's first arch, each portrait is underlined with two dolphins or dolphin like fish hooked together at the tails. They have the same majestic green as the scenes further inside the altar. It is difficult to appreciate something so intricate and the mosaics are so hidden and live on a ceiling in a narrow room that is awkward and difficult to look up at. They can only be glanced at overtime. Part of its appeal is knowing it is there. That it exists. You do your best to memorize the imagery with the hope you never forget all the perfectly placed columns and intricate designs. But you can never perfectly remember the patterns of the dresses of every pretty girl you see at a party. They are for the moment. Most of them, at least.

Groups of teenage school children are brought through and do their best to pay attention to the guide explaining the altar. But most only give a glance and begin to fidget. Somewhere in their mind, they know they are not capable of looking too long— it is not that they are badly behaved or do not care— they know how complex it is in the short time it takes to look up just once.

The altar is the largest of eight arches circulating beneath the dome. The others are more muted in their tone and design. Only a rough coat of paint. But they have a glorious position, so that enables more praise from me. The curves of the outer porticos are bare and free of any decoration. Their shape just as fascinating as the altar's colors and patterns, but they are simple and easily understood. In a church so large it almost seems an insult they do not have mosaics of their own. The light inside the church is minimal even in places where the walls do not need protection from light.

There is an element of this place being forgotten. Its age is resoundingly felt.

Any person turned off by the color of the mud brown brick of Ravenna's churches is pleasantly surprised by the charming colors upon stepping inside. Most especially, the outside of the Mauseoleum of Galla Placidia, which is a harsh contrast to its glittering interior. The same could be said for the Battistero Neoniano. Going inside is like cutting open a kiwi.

The little gated complex in which the Mausoleum and San Vitale are set is charming and made so by its manicured grass. The grass makes one appreciate the whole site all the more especially when walking towards the front gate to leave. The outside of the gate makes one sad just as it would be sad to leave the nicely manicured estate of a friend who possesses all the peaceful traits of a monk, merely concerned with the beauty and solitude of their patch of land.

The museum next door is a pleasant building to experience. The second inner courtyard had an almost nirvana-like peace and quiet. The large trees give the illusion that it is covered.

Ravenna is a wonderful place for strolling and the name Ravenna itself, swims in your mind the whole time you are there. After a short while it interchanges with the word 'river.' The streets take the shape of narrow waterways. If the flood were to come it could become a kind of toned-down Venice.

Ravenna is a secret of sorts, because it is not Rome or Venice as few places are, but Ravenna has been known and written about by Wilde and Henry James, Byron lived here for two years and Dante is buried here. A steady stroll through its curving streets is an epiphany of sorts, for it looks a secret because it is hardly spoken of. So quiet, so calm, without the hoards of those in a state of vacation.

I sat down tonight having spent the day admiring Ravenna's churches and mosaics, and the words of Henry James became even more poignant and vivid. I reread a lot of what he wrote about the city and through rereading I began to further appreciate it and the images sunk further into my eyes and into my mind— and of course I imagined James doing the same. I imagined Oscar Wilde doing the same— I imagined everyone who had ever been to Ravenna doing the same.

I had taken a number of notes inside the San Vitale and I noticed the resemblance to what James had wrote— when I reread them I did not picture him there quite as vividly as I did inside the Galla Placidia. The Galla Placidia is such a small building that nearly everyone who goes into it would have a similar reaction and experience the same feelings, and realize that "the shadow of the great Roman name still broods...and abides forever within."

February 11th   Modena

For a place so grand in every corner, the only thing it appears to be missing is people. It looks oddly sparse. There is too much attention to detail for Modena to be considered a secret or forgotten or abandoned. The rich reds make it an extension of Bologna— thus a kind of palace. Piazza Roma is certainly palatial. It is another place that appears overtly wealthy without ostentation.

I spent a few hours yesterday at the Lamborghini factory in Sant'Agata Bolognese and today at the Ferrari gallery in Maranello. Both are a perfect expression of modern Italy. It is not just ruins and aging architecture or centuries old painting and sculpture that comes out of Italy. These cars are a most modern kind of art that of course has been around in Italy for more than fifty years now. I watched as the Lamborghini workers put together each car by hand. Interiors hand stitched piece by piece. The hard and the delicate elements of a car, so seemingly different, only a room apart waiting to be conjoined. The large dyed cowhides were draped over tall benches. The guide spoke of how they only used very large cows from the north of Italy. It was easy to appreciate how they are more than just cars. They are works of art and ingenuity and are very much from, of and by Italy.

It was satisfying to hear how many of the workers usually remain there for life. And it is no surprise that

Lamborghini and Ferrari are largely made for foreigners. The world— in the newest and grandest way— wants what Italy has and creates. Hand made cars that look futuristic and are more awe inspiring in their design and function than any other. It does not seem too unreasonable to imagine one of those cars in the same gallery as a sculpture or paintings.

The latest addition of the 'Grand Tour' is a visit to Lamborghini and Ferrari. The modern traveler flocks to Maranello and Sant'agata Bolognese just like any other Italian or European place of cultural pilgrimage. The only thing more grand is to return home in one of the cars. Modernity does have a charming side, too.

February 12th   Ferrara

A waiter in Ravenna told me how snobbish and full of themselves the people of Ferrara can be, and when he said it is very cold I thought he was referring to the weather but he also meant the people. Perhaps this is not the best information to have in one's mind when arriving to a new place, but nonetheless you feel a difference of character in Ferrara. I initially got the sense it is a place resistant to change and somewhat insular, but as I sat outside of Al Brandisi beside the Duomo— American blues blasted from the six-hundred-year-old restaurant. And then a little while later as I dug into my Capellacci di Zucca an anciently dressed priest slowly walked past draped in a long black cape and a wide brimmed hat.

February 13th   Ferrara

The city's maturity is in its little old ladies with their well-coiffed hair and fur coats indulging at the cafés bordering the main piazza. They chomped indulgently on croissants.

There was a Monday market lining the southern wall of the city selling mostly used clothing— an unexpected sight. Fortunately, Monday means the museums are closed making it quite easy to enjoy a long walk atop the city walls. They are a colossal sight just like the walls of Lucca. I regret not roaming on Lucca's walls, but I was in a rush to get to Pisa. It is not every day one gets to walk on top of a nine-kilometer wall built a thousand years ago completely encircling the city. It is plain to see that it is more than a barrier— it does a great deal to shape the character of the city. Any barrier has a way of being breached. The wall is a frame to the city's portrait. Its eastern side is impossibly high and appears unbreachable. Its outer face is an intimidating army of bricks. It is hard and weathered and even though patches of bricks are missing, the wall shows no signs of weakening. On the city side of the wall, there is almost always a grassy hill that starts at street level and quickly slopes upward to the flat walkways on the top.

The wall is centuries old but today modernity is always nearby for nearly everything along the inside streets is a modern construction and the roads are filled with parked cars while others are loudly buzzing by. The northeast corner turns the wall into a bridge through a pleasant little forest. Oddly enough the outside is often far more appealing— for there is almost always a large grassy park with manicured trees and copious joggers taking advantage of the sidewalk that parallels the wall. At some parts on the top of the wall, its bricks below cannot be seen, and it feels like standing on the edge of a cliff. All that can be seen is green sloping down into the city on one side and green flattening out for a few hundred yards on the other. It is funny how the barrier's design makes one ignorant to its presence, perhaps it makes some ignorant to the security it is meant to provide. To the outsider, the walls of the city are brick but to the citizens they see no wall— they see grass, a city surrounded by hills and nature.

Ferrara is another castle like city and it is only fitting to find a castle fit with a moat in the center. Sparse and clean on the inside it appears brand new. Of course there was a tower and of course I climbed it. The view of the city that is not quite red. The roofs a faded red nearing a kind of light flesh tone. A city that does not have the need to show you how grand it really is.

February 14th   Parma

At Reggio Emilia this morning there were many African migrants. A seemingly disproportionate amount for such a small city like Reggio. There must have been a couple hundred and many with little to do but hang outside the train station. Near the piazzas in the center of the city they do their best to sell fake designer handbags. Setting up on a blanket for a few minutes before packing up and setting up again in another location to avoid the scouring of the police patrol. Almost all men— living in a hopeless situation. There is little to do. The women appear settled and pushed strollers. The men appear lost— like they don't know why they have come to Italy. Have they been sold a dream by smugglers?

Heat pumps through the vents of the floor of the Duomo's gilded interior. Plenty of visitors in groups and couples. But not a soul at Basilica di San Giovanni Evangelista behind the Duomo. Freezing cold and dark except for a blinding spotlight near the altar more suitable for the outside of a warehouse. The floors were tiled in the most interesting tricolor cubed pattern. It was dirty and clearly had been for a long time.

The Battistero's beautiful white and pink outside is almost as beautiful as the colorful arches of the ceiling. So narrow and high it is difficult to look for long.

February 15th   Parma

In Parma at the café the slang for cappuccino is Capucho.

I wondered if the river Parma always look as sad as it does today. A low river looks impotent, which makes the bridges look frivolous.

The greatest structure in Parma is set inside of another structure. It is not easy to say so because the beautiful Battistero is only a few streets away. The Teatro Farnese is Giovani Battista Alcotti's beautiful creation. It is a truly unique creation. How rarely does one see a stadium or entire amphitheater made of wood— let alone one that is inside. Though, it is inside it feels a colossal site. The outside somehow brought in. To enter on the ground floor through the center is to walk onto a stage. It is a peculiar and unique entrance for a theater. You are immediately immersed in a crowd you cannot entirely see. Its immensity is fully felt without anyone sitting in its benches.

The theater does its best to mislead you into believing you are outside and only the ceiling beams remind you that you are enclosed inside. Light beams through the side windows like Caravaggio's *The Calling of St. Matthew* in Rome. Every glance at the theater is a completely fresh look. I spent nearly an hour in there sitting, walking, and looking around in amazement. The curves guide you around and feel as though they move your neck for you. The alterations of light provide deception to its size and a few clicks of the neck or a few steps in one direction certainly bring back its immensity that was there all along.

Only kings and governments have the privilege to build such structures. It is a public show piece. Architecture is a most awesome art and structures like the Teatro Farnese inspire aesthetic bliss.

February 17th   Cremona

I passed through Piacenza this morning and had a few restful minutes in the deserted San Sisto Church. All of these churches are not just places of worship or centers of power. The church is a repository of art and design, because power so often enables art even in the smallest of places. The power and influence looks gone but the art and design remains, and the churches become a container of peace and quiet. So often they are empty and how easy it is to have them all to yourself. To find contentment and solitude in such places is most satisfying.

After seeing so many beautiful churches it would be easy to say that Cremona's Duomo is simply just one more, but it is dazzling and inspiring in so many ways. This abundance of beautiful architecture never gets old and I never fully get used to it. You do not expect it quite like you do expect food to taste delicious. There are always thrills and it excites you in new ways. Cremona's Duomo is so large you see it from more than a few streets away and all plans of wandering through Cremona's little streets are put on hold in order to take part in the satisfying activity of sitting across the piazza drinking coffee beneath the large stone porticos, always keeping the Duomo in sight.

It is February 17th, but the weather is more like March 17th, yet the Italians are still bundled up with large coats and wool hats like it is January 17th— and yet they still insist on strolling with their generous portions of gelato capped on a cone. So it is a lovely paradox— and all of this is subtle decoration to the life of the piazza. The further north in Italy I travel the larger the fur coats become and the smaller the old ladies wearing them. Their toy dogs seem to shrink as well. Dogs as accessory are serious business around here.

There was another tower to climb and the five hundred steps of the Salita al Torrazo led to an almost dizzying height. It was serene to reach its top level where you find not only another bell, but a lovely five o'clock sunset framing the city.

The Duomo's interior was covered with lots of aging greens. In many places it is a kind of weathered mint color. The kind of greens that can go terribly wrong if not put in the right setting or left to their own devices, say as a couch or a cocktail dress. But they are not alone, for the paintings over and under the arches and porticos busy your eyes and the spattering of gold brings a bit of seriousness to everything involved. In fact, the gold and the green play off each other surprisingly well.

It helps to like the name of something or someone in order to like it more. I very much think that about girlfriends and friends— it is so difficult to fall in love with Molly or Deirdre. I have been fortunate with my two girlfriends having such beautiful names, saying their names almost makes me miss them. I missed saying their names. There was something about the name Cremona that inspired a kind of bliss and contentment before having even seen the city. The name alone has had me wondering what Cremona was like for weeks. There are prettier names and perhaps if Cremona were the name of some town in southern Indiana it would be spoiled or wasted, but it always somehow makes everything much prettier to me.

February 18th   Cremona

Never before have I seen so many fur coats. Yesterday, I naïvely thought I had seen them all but today the old ladies were out in droves wearing the most puffy and gaudiest of furs in various colors and shapes and sizes. They are almost a ceremonial garb, but the religion being the daily routine of the lady— separating them from the other moderately dressed ladies of the town.

I spent some time at the unique museum dedicated to the violin. Such a beautiful thing even when it is not emanating a sound. The violin has an undoubtably erotic shape. It is a seductive little creation.

Cremona was covered in fog all day and it only thickened into the night, making the tower beside the Duomo disappear. Around the piazza there were more raucous drinkers than I had seen in Rome, Naples and Florence combined. I think they might have just been rowdy teenagers running around shouting. The fog increased and fell to the streets, the whole of the Duomo fading away. Cremona became a ghostly place.

February 19th   Mantua

This morning I woke up early and the streets were lined with the tables of people selling their antiques, furniture, books, records and junk. The streets were cluttered and the temperature had gone close to freezing. I preferred pastries to junk and sauntered into the pretty little pasticceria beside the Duomo then headed to the train station. It is difficult to resist the main dish of the region or rather these couple of regions in the north; Tortelli di Zucca. So far I find that Ferrara does it best in the form of Cappellacci di Zucca— which is more like a dumpling than a ravioli. And in Ferrara it is not just offered in butter and sage but can also be topped with ragu.

The Piazza Sordello had a cluttered junk and antique market just like Cremona, only larger. Some stalls were comically messy with paintings and frames in piles to be picked from. It made the rocky square all the more colorful.

I breezed through the Palazzo Ducale and found its surrounding lakes much more interesting. I had read an article about how it was the perfect place to get rid of a body and while looking out over the water I could only wonder how many people had been disposed of in those lakes, especially with a center of power like the Palazzo Ducale so close by.

I drank a cup of chocolate at a loud bar, came back to my little room and spent the night reading about Caravaggio.

February 20th   Mantua

Today is the 117th anniversary of the execution of Andreas Hofer, and as I stumbled into the Piazza Sordello this morning not fully awake and holding a little bag of fritelle, I was greeted by the sight of a few hundred men in full military dress. Men of all ages with eccentric facial hair dressed in traditional Tyrolean uniforms from the early 19th century to celebrate the occasion. Young women stood in obedience adorned in long puritanical dresses. They all lined up in the piazza in a concise formation and began to march to Piazza Mantegna in front of the cathedral where there was an inspection of the troops, and a band played. They then marched through the streets and all of the crowd walked alongside out of the center of the city towards Piazza d'Arco.

In a rocky courtyard surrounded by yellow buildings a few men gave speeches in German and Italian beside a painting of Andreas Hofer. The band played and *Zu Mantua in Banden*, the anthem of the Tyrol commemorating Hofer's struggle, was sung. In one of the German speeches, Trump and 'America First' were mentioned and so was ISIS. The mayor of

Mantua spoke— the band played again— all withstood the dull songs while a wreath was hung on a wall below a plaque commemorating Hofer. The plaque reads in Italian and German:

"To valiantly have defended his Tyrol he was tried here and sentenced to death by a Napoleonic Court on February 19, 1810."

His execution came a day later. His crime was leading a rebellion of the Tyrolean people against Napoleon's invading forces in 1809. He was captured and sent to Mantua. His execution was by firing squad for which he himself was to give the call to shoot. He refused a blindfold and refused to face the firing squad on his knees.

The distance from the city's outer most buildings to the shores of the lakes is much further than one assumes. It is a great separation. I was thinking again of the article I read of how it was a good place to get rid of a body. I again stood along the shore at night wondering just how many had been dumped into those lakes and it became an unsettling place.

If Mantua's center on a Monday night was not deserted— its shorelines were a Siberia. The tall narrow trees along the shore had no leaves and became spooky silhouettes. The lights that shine on the path only cover small spots and uselessly shine upwards as well as into your eyes. They are positioned as such to leave ten feet of shoreline completely black and even darker than the water, thus the shoreline looks like one long abyss. The path lights did little good other than filling anyone walking with the dread of being seen by a potential killer. There were times when the lights hinder the line of sight of anyone watching from afar and I felt safer standing in dark patches.

During the day from the lake's shore the Palazzo Ducale looks a benign pile of stone. But at night the lights shooting from the ground up the outer walls and its porticos fully lit, turning the palazzo to a symbol of torture and the house of a tyrant.

There are no boats venturing out for a nighttime jaunt on the lakes— they are as deserted as the shorelines and Mantua feels as though it is set on a cliff. The long stretches of unhindered road that form a ring around the city enable cars to drive very fast as if it were a highway. It creates another barrier between the city and its shoreline— discombobulating anyone walking along the road and further isolating the shoreline. The bridge going across the water at Mantua's northern tip looks like a highway going through a border crossing to another country.

Up close to the palazzo all the lights are large and blinding so as to properly showcase the building but from the walls to the street there are large patches of black and you cannot see anything directly at eye level. At the wall, it is a long drop down to the shallow moat and the faded stone where the water once was looks like an exposed foundation. It is the only part of the building that looks vulnerable.

The lighting of Mantua is decidedly odd. There are large blinding lights beaming down or across at weird angles so that the streets take the form of an empty film set designed for a murky mob hit— with the sound of expensive shoes clicking on the street from shadowy figures.

February 21st   Padua

I had to backtrack on trains via Brescia, but I enjoyed the extra time on the trains to look at the empty countryside blanketed in a spooky white fog. The leafless trees were always set against the fog and each branch and twig was made all the more vivid.

The area around the train station was unwelcoming. There were shady men on every corner in the surrounding area staring long at whomever passed by.

The Capella degli Scrovegni sits in a gated little park beside a busy road. One can only imagine its charms hundreds of years ago when its setting was even quieter and more surrounded by nature. It is another chapel like a kiwi, the common brick exterior with a deliciously colorful interior. The ceiling is mostly a beautiful blue and the most prominent color of the whole chapel. The circular portraits stare back at you. If only the interior of every church had such a soothing color. This blue is so rare it is almost exclusive or a kind of secret. Both the painters and the churches commissioning designs with this blue are bold in comparison to some more conservative church designs.

The depictions of hell are always more interesting than those of heaven and convey madness more than anything. Everyone not in hell is serene and calm— and quickly forgotten by those looking from the chapel floor. The small group of people buzzes at one point near the depictions of hell. All of the frescoes are skillfully done and are better than most I have seen.

February 22nd   Padua

I prefer the outside of the Palazzo Ragiorne to its upper floor interior, which looks an oversized basketball gym in the Midwest or the Park Avenue Armory. The frescoes are undoubtably beautiful but somewhat spoiled by their setting. I came to find they were a replacement for some lost Giotto paintings. The size of the building turns them to championship banners in a high school, but there are far too many and a school that wins that much would be far too indifferent to displaying them. But they are really there to influence the judges that once worked there when it was used as a court and for other kinds of law administration. The scenes reminded judges of the common tendencies and characteristics of human beings and therefore sought to encourage the most just verdicts.

It is a hollow space when it is left to merely be admired. It is made all the more weird by the presence of an oversized four-hundred-year-old wooden horse statue at one end. The horse was once used as a prop in performances of *The Trojan Horse* and the actors would come out of the horse's belly.

February 23rd   Venice

I quickly fell in love with a girl from Marsala, Sicily named Gessica— yes with a G. She hated having to live and work in Venice. She could not care less about all the beauty. Her love and loyalty was to Sicily. She had no choice, she was Sicilian, not Venetian.

At the Chiesa Santa Maria del Giglio— in the chapel there is a most beautiful Rubens painting entitled, *Virgin and Child with the Infant St. John*.

I was here eight years ago and did not enjoy a minute of it. The place was covered in fog and so was I. But today is different. I could not be happier to be in the Most Serene Republic of Venice, La Serenissima. I am surrounded by beauty. The streets are made of water, everything is floating, even me.

February 25th   Venice

Since I got to Venice I have found myself not wanting to say much or write much, and all I really wanted to do was look and enjoy being here. Riding along in a water taxi down the Grand Canal is a simple yet serenely happy experience that quickly fills me with content.

I have not been taking copious notes like I did in every little town and city throughout Italy. It has been more pleasurable to just sit back and enjoy this place, for how often does one get to spend more than a few days gliding and strolling and of course floating around this magical city.

Though, today I slowly pushed myself to take some notes as I want to remember more than just the feeling of Venice.

Venice's uglier, poor and more forgotten sections around the ghetto are there and do not really inspire the same way the Grand Canal does and mostly remind you of the common Venetian still living a hard working existence in the city. It reminds you that life is not glittering and beautiful everywhere— and is often nearby to the places that do glitter, but you leave those sections like you would leave any other place and make your way back to more inspiring places like San Marco or by the opening to the lagoon.

Yesterday, I went through the Palazzo Ducale, including the secret rooms and prisons upstairs—

Casanova was a prisoner and managed to escape. It was interesting to find that even the graffiti covered cells have beautifully curved ceilings. A sinister rope hung from the ceiling to a small set of stairs in the middle of the room designated for torture. In front was a desk with three chairs for interrogators to ask questions and bark orders from.

The more I heard about the governments of Venice over the centuries I could not help but think how reasonable and democratic they sounded. There was always an anti-establishment thread running through the elite and powerful. The Venetian Republic seemed an intelligent one. They would have to be a thoughtful people in order to govern and organize a city so constantly faced with matters of the sea and water. Living on water requires one to almost constantly think about it. Its endless motion and sounds, and of course its potential hazard. Water makes for a thoughtful mind.

Today, I read Joseph Brodsky's most perfect little book, *Watermark*. When thinking of the intelligence and success of the Venetian republic I could not help but consider Brodsky's lines about traveling on water being primordial and also being reminded through the feelings in your feet rather than the other senses that one is out of place when on the water.

Perhaps some of the tourists scream with joy or shriek with delight upon seeing and being in Venice but for me it very much quiets me down and I feel an internal ease— there was not much weight to lift off of my shoulders to begin with but if there was any, it had certainly disappeared.

Come to think of it I have not even thought of something like anxiety while being here or even had a simple worry— I have not been worried about falling in the water—perhaps I should— and I am not bothered in the least by the pushy crowds of San Marco Square or the gridlocked streets.

I have come to find it somewhat difficult to complain about tourists in Venice like all those travel snobs love to do because in Venice you know they are what keep the city alive to a certain extent. I do not think the disdain for tourists in Venice is entirely truthful— I think mostly it comes from a wish to have Venice be what it once was, and that is always an unreasonable desire.

Not all tourists in Venice are of the cruise ship type, day-trippers from the mainland or flying in for a weekend from somewhere in Europe. It is clear that during Carnevale you see the people who truly love Venice— so devoted to the life and culture and beauty of Venice. They spend thousands of dollars to dress as Venetians once did hundreds of years ago.

They do not just come to gawk with entranced faces at Venice— but to be looked at behind a mask, in capes and oversized hair and dresses in the square, streets, hotel lobbies— and the most random places become an outdoor gallery for people putting

Venetian style on display. Perhaps there is a strain of the self-centered and narcissistic in them, but they are undoubtably Romantics. They do not do Carnevale anywhere quite like Venice. It may be a more raucous party in Rio de Janeiro or New Orleans, but Venice's Carnevale has more than an air of maturity and sophistication and of course, fun. There are hardly any drunk people to be found— a drunk is a strange occurrence for Venice. The serenity of the city provides a certain more preferable kind of intoxication.

The tourists also serve a purpose for the non-tourist type— they show you what much of the well to do world looks like all at once— American, western European, Japanese and Chinese for the most part. I laughingly thought, they are not like me. They are mostly people restricted by their time— whether it is their own fault or someone else's. They are the locals of somewhere else. Snobs only like locals when they stay put.

Looking down at all this water and essentially living with it you get a better sense of what a great flood is, what it means, and you do not feel as afraid of the talk of rising sea levels. I began to entertain the thought of Manhattan flooding and transforming into a kind of gridded Venice. The streets could be torn out, the subway ripped up-- the underbelly of Manhattan could handle a great deal of water— but the face of the city would obviously change— it would move at a Venice like pace, but perhaps somewhat quicker because of all the wide avenues and linear streets. The idea of a flood in Manhattan makes you realize how small Venice is.

I recently re-watched the *Vidal in Venice* documentary and re-read the book and my favorite line was that in the whole history of Venice there have only been three million Venetians— which sort of makes one's mind spin with wonder. A wonderful fact. It makes Venice seem as though it is an exclusive place, but how could a place so grand reach such power with so few people? I think that statistic says a lot to the intelligence, ingenuity and ambition of the people of Venice— not just of a single generation but over centuries of a people naturally inclined toward success.

On the island of Giudecca, it is so quiet it is as though it is an island for quarantine or isolation. One or two ladies walk their dogs but quickly return to one of the ugly modern apartment blocks once the dog has done its business. From every balcony hangs clothing and on more than one hangs the neon colored clothing of the policemen and sanitation workers of Venice. I had noticed them quietly patrolling and cleaning San Marco Square with homemade Witch-like brooms or dealing with difficult tourists in one capacity or another— it was natural to see them in the square but to find their uniforms drying in the wind of these depressing apartment blocks humanized them and took them out of the background of the city. Compared to the tourists there are so few of them they look lost. It was a peculiar sight to see those clothes for it was obvious who they belonged to. But it also made me think that Venetians for the most part go unnoticed, perhaps naturally because there are fewer and fewer of them each year.

The dead are important to the life of any city and Venice would be incomplete without the cemetery of Isola di San Michele. It is a rather dreamy idea for the sole purpose of a small island to be the resting place for the city's dead and for Venice it is particularly fitting. The island viewed from Venice's quieter northern edge is situated a short vaporetto ride away. As one approaches Isola di San Michele, the sight of its fortress like walls exudes an air of ceremony, properly preparing one for the sudden presence of a few thousand grave sites. From the cemetery's grounds, the sea is hidden by the island's protective walls and can only be seen from its few entrances.

It is a tranquil place to wander, beneath a blue sky and the sounds of the sea are never far. I did my best to find Ezra Pound in the simple gravestone etched only with his name that lay beside Olga under some messy shrubs. The section reserved for non-Catholics is messier and forgotten compared to the section reserved for Venetians, but it is not surprising, as the graves of Venetians are busily tended to by relatives and friends.

The island cemetery is a fitting resting place for Venetians and the foreigners who lived and loved in

Venice. Venetians are forever living with the presence of water and just like the palazzos and small apartments of Venice, the cemetery walls give the pleasant illusion of being in an ordinary city. Even though there are fewer and fewer Venetians they have always lived closely amongst each other in life as well as in death, still defying the dangers of water that surround them but not the ultimate force of time. In Venice, water is always present the same way death is always nearby, and Venetians approach both in the same way, by staying with family on the islands of the lagoon.

February 26th   Venice

Isola di San Michele is not the only cemetery of the Venice lagoon. There is also the Burano cemetery situated on the island next to Burano called Mezzorbo. On a Sunday— the cemetery's outer pink walls were a pleasant and inviting sight much like the colorful buildings of Burano. Inside, elderly people and their families devoted to the dead were dotted around the graves to water flowers and clean the colorful plaques of the deceased that are set into each gravestone and tomb. Sets of staircases on wheels sit in front of the above ground tombs that stack up to six graves high. The Venetians politely ignore the few gawking foreigners. Pairs of old ladies speak secretively in the corners of the cemetery.

The small graves of children who lived for one day are particularly sad. After seeing them the cemetery became a darker shade and the elderly couple meticulously cleaning a marble grave nearby was a much more touching scene that no longer looked an eccentric habit or ritual, but an act of love and continued grief.

Mezzorbo and Burano are quiet little islands and if it were not for its brightly colored homes you would not think much other than lacemaking goes on there. But the cemetery and those cleaning the graves show you there is life, love, loss, grief and devotion on this distant part of the Venice lagoon.

February 27th   Venice

When I got off the boat at Lido, I kept walking until I was all the way down by the little canals at Malamocco, where I sat beside the lagoon to finish Henry James' *The Aspern Papers*. Between the last few chapters I took time to glance out at Poveglia, the abandoned plague island, which appeared to float, for the horizon was covered in a white fog and the sky was a clear blue. Poveglia is supposedly haunted, but from my perspective it was a beautiful little spot.

February 28th   Venice

In the narrow streets, the trash-men pulled carts from door to door ringing each bell. The trash boats wait at a nearby bridge.

I went through the Accademia and the Museo Correr stopping for coffee in the cafe of the latter to take in the pleasant view over San Marco Square. The only continuous thing about the main sights of San Marco Square is their individual beauty and magical design— each standing out in its own unique way. The line was much too long to get into St. Mark's today, so hopefully I will have better luck tomorrow. St. Mark's is so odd it is easy to come to the conclusion that those constructing and refurbishing it over the centuries have had a consistently mischievous sense of humor. It is possibly the most un-Christian looking cathedral there is. It looks less a cathedral and more like the house of a mad wizard king. In this most un-Islamic city, the large domes give more than an impression of that not too distant religion. Each dome is capped with another onion shaped dome, making it all the more random and playful, like a boy wrapping himself in a potpourri of his parents' much too large clothing.

It is a pleasure to get lost in Venice's labyrinthine streets and always difficult to fully know how to get around. Outside the Grand Canal most every street and small canal is a new and confusing sight and only upon reaching one of the small piazzas can you get a sense of which direction you have been walking. The buildings appear much higher and crush your sense of direction, blocking the light causing temperatures to suddenly change and when you think you are almost where you want to be you have to climb up and then down the stairs of a bridge and snake your way back in a completely different direction. If it were not for the flow of crowds and yellow signs for San Marco or Rialto it would be nearly impossible for most to get anywhere in a timely manner on foot without a map.

March 1st   Venice

Today I looked at my phone and sent a message to someone I had never met. It was a girl named Pia. I sent her a message perhaps for one part curiosity, one part loneliness, and one part for the urge to do a lot of talking. She was in Venice for a day and for some reason she responded— so we met in San Marco Square and quickly walked past the cathedral and into the busy streets to get lost. She held a bright multi-colored Yves Saint Laurent bag that was difficult to remove my eyes from and seemed a one of a kind treasure one receives from a King. She was chic and confident with her large sunglasses, bubbly winter coat and beautiful black hair, as well a pleasure to talk to as we navigated the crowds and got lost in the streets.

We were two strangers talking and joking and sharing the collective pleasure that comes with turning the corner of most any street in Venice. At the Rialto Bridge, a Labrador Retriever sat beside his owner with a paw firmly wrapped across his chest to hug him. It looked a particularly beautiful scene one could only find in Italy and perhaps most fittingly in Venice, where the beauty piles on top of itself and one has to almost learn how to consume so much beauty all at once. We found small intimate piazzas that no tourists were anywhere near including one with a row of old expensive champagne bottles on a dirty ledge. The bottles were more than twenty years old and could easily have been taken as souvenirs or smashed by some mischievous teenagers, but they remained for they were difficult not to appreciate like most things in Venice. Pia pointed out that they were stained from the months and likely years of rain.

Eventually we made our way to the Fondamente Nove to look out at Isola di San Michele and we could see it framed between the buildings before we got to the end of the street. It was brightly lit from a setting sun that shined directly onto its southern walls.

When we sat down at Harry's it was still too early for dinner, but we drank Bellinis and talked about business, comedy and family for so long that we stayed for dinner which gave us the same feeling that everything in Venice did for us, pleasure. Fabulous old ladies would come in one at a time dressed in large puffy furs and jewelry. They wore expensive outfits to have dinner with their just as extravagantly dressed friends. They ate well, as much as a hungry teenage boy would. They ate more than us.

Pia's face only became more striking now that it was no longer covered with sunglasses and since we sat beside each other in a corner we were not always looking at each other as we drank, ate, laughed and took in the scene. But when we did, I could hardly not notice her dark brown eyes that became greenish whenever they were hit with a stroke of light. When we looked at each other I was reminded that we had only just met a few hours before and forced myself not to look too long, but when listening and talking to each other I got the sense that I had sat with Pia before. The ease of the conversation reminded me that all good conversation has a similar thread running through it and makes you feel as though you have been there before even with someone you have just met. All good conversation was somehow linked together.

We were greeted by Harry himself who was dressed sharply in a double-breasted suit, red shirt and a colorful tie. Everything about him was charming.

We walked into San Marco Square under a dark sky where we had met only a few hours earlier still chatting just as much. But then we walked back towards our hotels. On the Calle Seconda de l'Ascension we quickly hugged each other, said we would keep in touch and then said goodbye.

I had spent the first half of the day wandering through Venice and even got into St. Mark's Cathedral when the line had died down. By the early afternoon I thought Venice had given me a most complete day. I aimed to fill the rest of the afternoon with a few hours of reading followed perhaps by some more wandering through Venice's streets with a ride down the Grand Canal, but after we said goodbye I realized that no day in Venice is complete without telling a pretty girl about your whole life, nor is it complete without hearing most everything about hers, too.

March 4th   Vicenza

Leaving Venice made me realize what a bubble the city is. How unreal and unlike any other place. I had gotten used to its streets and canals perhaps as much as one could in a week. The Veneto was covered in a gray rainy sky which made the grass surrounding its bare vineyards a rich green. I had to acclimate to the sight of so much green and had almost forgotten how pretty it can be.

At the café in the Cornuta station the lady with the oversized lips was not interested in helping me get a taxi to Villa Maser. The café was crowded with local men talking up a storm and almost completely disappointed by the sight of me, a foreigner, coming through the door. Though, the nice man who owned the place gave me a number to call and soon after I was further out in the country and inside one of Palladio's greatest creations. It is difficult not to be distracted by the colossal church that sits in the village just before the villa. Another Palladian creation.

The rain quickly forced me under the porticos of the villa, and I wondered whether I was in the right place. I could not make out the shape I had seen in all the pictures of Maser and the girl selling tickets held back her laughter when I asked if I was at Villa Maser.

Starting at the best of anything has its downsides but with Palladio one comes to find that the best of Palladio's villas is a matter of opinion. I quickly realized that the beauty of Palladio lies in its simplicity. Everywhere one looks, is with the eye of the designer. You can see the artist at work, always careful not to do too much. Like a sculpture, Palladian villas, especially Maser, appear carved out of stone, rather than stones staked upon each other.

Maser is still very much a private home even with a couple dozen noisy visitors traipsing about in oversized slippers covering their shoes. The layout of Villa Maser may be simple, but the excess of the villa is found in its Veronese Frescoes. One would think this is too much for a home, but as grand as they appear, they are a natural fit to the villa and many miles from ostentation. The large windows of the villa have views out to the vineyards and the surrounding landscape and behind the villa to the curvaceous Nymphaeum.

Wherever one is positioned in Villa Maser they are treated to a view of complete and utter beauty.

The fat rain kept Maser's gardens empty, but I ventured down the rocky walkway with my bag over my head as an insufficient umbrella to get a view of the whole of the villa. Gradually, the center of the villa that protrudes further than the rest, sunk backwards and for one's eyes it was a subtle magic trick in reverse. A revealed illusion had become concealed. You do not see Villa Maser until you see it from the gate by the road and from far out in the vineyards. A complete view of Villa Maser from a distance is all one would need to consider it a work of art on par with any painting, sculpture, or piece of music of exception.

By the time I got to Vicenza it was dark and still raining and I must have walked past half a dozen Palladian buildings.

March 5th   Vicenza

La Rotonda was not open yet so I continued down the road into the vineyards following the signs for Villa Guicelli. I climbed the deep wooden staircase up through the ample forest and arrived at the villa, now a Risorgimento museum, which easily could have been reached by road or a more simple and less strenuous walk through the other side of Vicenza.

The church of St. Mary of Mount Barico was so full of worshipers that no one else could get through the doors on either side. Televisions broadcasted the service for parts of the church without a view of the altar. From the distant vineyards the church looked like the isolated castle of a mad king, like Neuschwanstein Castle, I was happily surprised to find it so filled with life and not a crazy Bavarian.

Vicenza's bells ring in the form of a song which I could not make out, but they are much more pleasant to hear than the typical damning monotone chime of so many other cathedrals. There is a lovely porticoed walkway that slopes downward beside the street. Palladio is everywhere.

Villa Valmarana ai Nani was a further reminder of Palladian simplicity. Still a private home, the owner's family pictures and possessions in plain view made for a feeling of trespassing.

At the Teatro Olympico, I spoke with a man named Pio from Puglia. We talked about the mafia and corruption in the south as that was what seemed to be on his mind, before we turned to the influence of Palladio on Jeffersonian architecture in Virginia. I remember buying Palladio's *Four Books of Architecture* when I visited Monticello. I told Pio to visit Virginia. He was eager to do so.

I expected the setting of La Rotonda to be in the middle of a vast sloping hill, but its surrounding walls are never far from the villa making it seem an elephant locked in a cage— the land only stretches far beneath its eastern wall through vineyards towards a highway. La Rotonda is a grand yet simple creation, and of course beautiful. Again I felt the beauty of Palladio's work was derived greatly from its simplicity. Also, I think height is a great factor in Palladian architecture— height inspires, intimidates, imposes— certainly a structure that is just the right height inspires even more. Palladian villas are large but never oversized— Palladio always gets that right. They do not stretch on forever and ever with bedroom after bedroom and servants quarters, salons etc. In this way, as palatial as Palladian villas are— they are ultimately accessible in the minds of all.

March 6th   Verona

I had the most extraordinary plate of tortelli filled with ricotta in a duck ragu and red wine sauce. Along with it I got a whole cup shaped portion of ricotta to mix with apple mustard, which is like honey and apples made spicy.

I guess I have little choice but to say that Verona is a perfect setting for Romeo and Juliet. Why try to think of it set anywhere else? Why avoid it? There is a lovely curvaceous river and plenty of colorful buildings and thousands of little stones that make up the surface of the street.

In the Basilica di Sant Anastasia, one happily finds a painted ceiling that is a garden of color with all of its twirling flowers— and can only further the romantic charm of Verona. The flowers draped down the porticoed ceilings and you reach out to touch them. It makes you realize the green—a natural grassy type— of the vines and stems is very much a color of romance. More than one initially thinks. It is the color of most of Verona's window shutters accenting many of the buildings. It is the color beneath a rose.

I found myself pondering the shape of Piazza della Erbe. It is unusual and perhaps formed naturally rather from some preconceived plan, but in a city so drenched in romantic thought there's something to be taken from the fact that its main square is shaped like a coffin.

March 7th   Verona

Though the city lives on both sides of the river, Verona's peninsula-like center surrounded by water looks an island like the Île-Saint-Louis when viewed from the banks of the river. The river is low but fast moving and sounds like a quietly running faucet. A city within a city— in a small way like Manhattan. Without its seven bridges Verona is very much an isolated little place.

March 8th   Sirmione

It was most definitely spring this afternoon at the end of the Sirmione peninsula for the birds filled the trees with their mating calls. In the garden of the grotto they covered all patches of grass but were scared and would make a thunderous sound whenever they felt approaching footsteps on the gravelly paths.

I sat for an hour or two at the tip of the peninsula, and it was quiet except for the waves of the lake and the chirping of birds. No one else had the idea to walk out this far, so looking out at all of the lake and all of the surrounding mountains made it seem it was all there just for me— like it was placed there and all I had to do was find it.

Every day in Italy has felt like the continuation of a long indulgent culture binge. Sometimes I worry what it will feel like when the binge comes to an end.

I finished the day sitting at the edge of an empty street that ended at the lake's shore and watched the sky turn orange, pink, purple and then black.

March 9th   Bergamo

It was a delightfully sunny day that could only mean it is Spring in Italy. That makes two days in a row.

I walked down to the Academy through the cobblestone streets and buildings. Raphael and Botticelli were the best of the lot yet again, I concluded, and then climbed back up the hill to the city. Bergamo somewhat reminds me of Perugia. A fortress but unworn by time— even the restorations look perfectly authentic.

Not an inch of the Basilica's ceiling is without a glittering detail. It is nearly impossible to count how many people are depicted in sculpture and painting on the ceiling alone. Its black and white checkered floor is somewhat baffling, but almost any organized pattern would do beneath such a ceiling so heavily covered with art.

At night I caught some beautiful glimpses of the colorful sky and horizon between the buildings, which led me to the edges of the city walls to look out at a sky turned pink and purple— a sky that can only be imagined.

March 10th   Bergamo

It is even more resoundingly Spring in Italy. That makes three days. After a nice little morning macchiato I walked west into the neighborhoods along the cliff that curves around just enough to look back at the whole of the center of Bergamo perched on the other side of the cliff.

I had two bowls of creamy polenta, one with Bergamo sausage and the other topped with a wild boar ragu. The first tasted fragrant, like an edible perfume.

I spent much of the rest of the day in and around the Piazza Vecchio which is the loveliest little crossroads there ever was. It is an eclectic bunch of buildings that do not seem to match. The square's quaint size makes for an intimate setting and doubled by the most tranquilly mature scene of coffee drinkers and girls singing beside a man plucking on a large bass. Never was there a voice too loud or a character out of line.

The square was a crossroads for the prettiest Italian girls with the most effortlessly feminine faces. Alone, in pairs and groups they passed through holding their violin cases in their arms with calm elegant expressions.

March 11th   Milan

I am very pleased to be in this endless slab of concrete. I was energized enough just from the very magnitude of the Stazione Centrale to walk nearly two miles to the center. I feel relieved to be in a city as large as this. I will never be bored. I will never struggle to find something entertaining or amusing.

I stumbled upon the renowned Peck restaurant and had a glowing plate of saffron risotto and traded glances with the pretty hostess.

March 12th   Milan

I tried to walk into *The Last Supper,* but the tickets were sold out for a week, so I happily settled for Caravaggio's *Dinner in Emmaus.* Sometimes one must settle for Caravaggio. Perhaps that can only be said in Italy.

March 13th   Milan

Monday amongst the Milanese. All the Milanese look unhappy on their way to work stuffed into the wretched orange tram cars. The trams are depressingly outdated and carry around people in the most up to date outfits. The sound of shrieking metal is maddening and often inescapable. To get anywhere quickly you have to listen to the sound of metal shriek.

I strolled down by the canals last night, a Sunday which felt like Friday and all the women were so beautiful, it was almost as if it was a contest to see whose pants could be tighter or look more fashionable. Every other woman looks like a runway model thus the men look much cooler than those who are model-less. The Italians have the most pronounced hairlines I have ever seen, nearly reaching down to the middle of their forehead. They are cool and everything around them is cool— but when you listen in, the conversations are almost always gossipy trash or tired political rants about the evils of McDonald's and Coca-Cola. It is all surface and shallow.

Milan is indifferent to the scorn it receives from traveling snobs and the aesthetically obsessed. It is going to go on being big and modern and continue to sprawl without any regard for character or charm. There is so much life behind all this concrete that ironically Milan does not care about the surface of itself.

March 14th   Milan

I had no desire to wait in line at the Duomo. Each day the line was longer no matter how unreasonably early I arrived. Milan was becoming busier each day and that meant Italy was getting busier, too. Every day the sky was more richly blue with not a single lingering cloud.

It was Spring and for the first time I felt like fleeing Italy, even though Milan gave me thoughts of getting a little job and a small apartment and staying for a while— for it would soon not be a place bereft of all the world's curious day trippers. There is hardly a place left to go. I had gone from Rome to Palermo to Venice and now far into the north.

So often have I struggled not to write how I have had a church, a piazza, a painting or a view all to myself but one can never have too much of Italy to their self.

March 15th   Milan

I crammed in for a coffee at Marchesi before a nice long walk down to Novigli again. The little Marchesi was filled with devoted patrons in suits and even firemen in full uniform happily drinking espresso with great care. How charming it is to see a fireman carefully holding a fine porcelain espresso cup with two fingers.

At Novigli the sight of water was pleasant, especially when it runs through the canal. It makes the city seem a part of nature. In the daytime I can more fully or more clearly see how shallow and dirty some of the canals are and how filled they are with beer bottles and random debris like umbrellas, cutlery and lighters. A few lost fish appear to swim as if they have survived a nuclear blast and somehow ended up in these dirty canals.

When I was walking around with Pia in Venice she had told me how the canals in Milan were littered with bottles. I never expected there to be so many. Most have sunk but you find a couple floating and others stuck into the bottom of the canal standing straight up. It is a reminder of Milan's unapologetically urban character. Everything is bound to be polluted. Nothing can hide.

The further out or the further south I walked along the canals the fish grew and so did the debris— Stop signs still attached to a pole and sections of a chain-link fence were jarring sights in the water that was now darker and more desperate. The further one walks the more graffiti covers the buildings, the more modern the buildings become, and one assumes they are in a sunny part of East Berlin. The city has less and less of a face and everything is neutral in character— apartment buildings look like warehouses with balconies or office buildings with balconies. Milan proves that modernity knows no bounds and even the Italians cannot resist it.

Milan is so wholeheartedly devoted to the church of urbanization that its churches are secluded and often unnoticeable. You find simple brick colored churches even where *The Last Supper* is housed. Because the churches are overwhelmingly brick they lack in importance and grandeur. Who prays in Milan?

Yet, the Duomo is a magical centerpiece taking on an almost foreign presence to its surroundings. But it is so magnificent it would be difficult for any city to stand next to it.

Without the Duomo the city is nearly without a face and could be a number of other latinized cities. São Pãolo and Santiago come to mind.

March 16th   Como

At Como the sun glows more than it shines through the thin layers of fog that coat most everything rising from the lake's shores.

The train was full of schoolchildren. My assumption that Como was a quiet lakeside town was only slightly realized. If only it were a secret. The park at the lake's edge is spoiled by the people who linger in it. Shady characters and homeless loiter and the Italian kids filled the air with weed.

March 17th   Cernobbio

The silky water of the lake appears black, like black rock covered with a liquid coating. There is a mystical fog looking north outlining the following mountains.

One of the few times I have ever enjoyed the sound of a guitar on a street was walking off the morning boat at Cernobbio onto the quiet dock. The man played for himself. I walked through the town and through the gates of Villa d'Este. It was like walking onto someone's private estate. I was supposed to be in a car and the guard at the gate was both suspicious and confused. I found it amusing to walk instead of drive to one of the world's most sought after hotels.

I took the bus up to Lenno and walked up the path to Villa Balbianello. A beautiful place that seems like the most perfect setting in all the world. You think it is impossible for something to be that beautiful. You become accustom afterwards and expectant of all things to be as beautiful. It is one of the most perfect homes in all the world.

I did not want to wait twenty minutes for the little boat taxi and decided to climb the winding little path pebbled with T-shaped stones that led to a small road that leads into a little forest on the lake, filled with whistling birds rummaging through the leaves. I quickly realized that though the road was tranquil it was a much more strenuous walk than I had assumed. The peninsula quickly feels like an island separated from the shores of the lake.

The villa had a lovely little library that had two secret doors, one that went downwards to a secret exit and the other up to the top floor of the library.

The last owner, Guido Manzino, has his collections dotted around the house. Sculptures and masks from all over the world as well as climbing memorabilia and souvenirs and gear from Manzino's mountain climbing career and explorations. He went to the north pole in 1971 and climbed Mount Everest in 1973. The villa looks the perfect place to recuperate after a long arduous journey.

The lake does much of the work to give the house a perfect view from every room. As good as each view is, it is easy to imagine that there are several days and weeks each year when the lake provides an even more perfect view. It is more perfect than an ocean view for as large as the lake appears it is an intimate setting.

I took the fast boat to Bellagio and ate some snails before wandering around the peninsula for a couple hours. The ride back to Como was a straight shot after Argegno. The speed of the boat makes you understand the lake's immense size. So many colorful houses simply shaped like cubes and upright rectangles, any detour from the typical style is a sore sight.

I sat on the back terrace of Villa d'Este writing and overlooking the lake as the twilight turned to night, the birds whistled like playful people would in a game of hide and seek. The lower parts of the mountains became peppered with gold dots that shiver without staring long at them and the slight fog remained. The mountain was silhouetted beneath the sky and no longer looked a mountain but an odd black horizon that comes with the night beside a lake such as this. The lights of the ferries still thundered down the lake and look more like hovercrafts than boats.

It is a wonder that armies and their leaders, like Napoleon, would capture something like this place and still feel inclined to seek other lands. Even this is not enough for some people. Perhaps seeking other places is some kind of flaw in many of us.

March 18th   Cernobbio

I took the bus again up the western shore and this time got off at Villa Carlotta to walk around the gardens for an hour before heading to Varenna for lunch. Varenna is beautiful and quiet from the approach just as it is from within.

Bellagio is a pleasant sight and more so when looking at it rather than from it. To look at it dead on from the north it looks a bubble or something that grew out of the earth rather than the work of man. Italians clearly do good work.

March 19th   Cernobbio

Villa d'Este is a mansion and even when there are more than a few drinkers on the rear terrace overlooking the lake it feels a private residence. I walked through the gate and into the town for coffee, then sat for a while near the pier writing and enjoying the view. I had lunch up at Gatto Nero, where they gave me a large wine glass of champagne upon sitting down. They do things with food that leave you speechless. A beautiful view.

I wandered into the gardens of the villa, past Hercules and up into the cliffs. On the rear terrace I wrote some more but mostly continued reading Casanova's memoirs which I had bought in Venice. I seem to be surrounded by some of the richest things life has to offer. Reading about the adventures of Casanova only enhances that. Everything in Italy is some kind of a dessert, and for me I would say it is a cake.

Chuck Berry passed away yesterday, so it only felt right to listen to him and look out over the lake. It was a good day to turn thirty-two.

March 20th   Stresa

It was a jumbled tangle of knots changing trains in Milan, heading south to head north again towards Lake Maggiore. All the trains moved slowly, and the Italians were as reserved as could be— barely making any sounds.

The train paralleled Maggiore as soon as it reached its southern most point and it was a tranquil sight the rest of the way to Stresa. Its shores are much further apart than Como, and its character was that much less intimate, but most any lake is a soothing presence no matter its shape or size.

If the water of Como appears black, Maggiore's was resoundingly blue— a blue eyed lake.

I had a sudden feeling of nostalgia for every moment that was suddenly not the present. A heightened sense of where I was, that I was indeed in Italy and that this was an inarguably good thing. I do not want it to end, yet I cannot wait to be looking back at it, knowing how good of a memory it will be. A part of traveling well is knowing a good memory when it is happening.

March 21st   Verbania

The lake was blanketed with fog this morning. The boat stopped briefly in Isola Bella and Isola Superiore dei Pescatori. I spent about an hour on each island. It was too early in the year and too early in the morning for anything other than a few cafés to be open. The gardens were closed but still a pleasant sight to see from the boat— the terraces and statues overlooking the lake.

In the middle of Isola Superiore was a miniature cemetery the size of a garden surrounded by a church and some little houses. I took note of one gravestone that had an outline of the African continent on it beside the man's name— Ernesto de Simone 1925–2012. I wondered about his life.

I arrived in Pollanza to a large crowd in front of a stage where spectators spoke loudly at an anti-mafia rally.

Even in this little town that already looked and felt like Switzerland, the mafia remained a force to be fought and resisted. All of the lakeside villas looked like Swiss chalet's and the boat ride like a border crossing, but the border was still further up the lake. It seems as though I have already left Italy. This place looks much different than the country I have been in for the last four months.

I walked down the road that was set on a cliff above the lake to Villa Taranto and got pleasantly lost in its gardens for some time.

March 22nd   Milan

The road to Switzerland was closed not far past Verbania and no boats were willing to cross the border, so I decided to come back to Milan and take the easier route of a simple train ride to Zürich. It would prove not to be as charming of an exit as I had imagined. But I do not mind for I feel at home in this colossal city and the train from Milan will be swift.

My journey had long been complete and much of the last few weeks have been icing on the cake. I feel more awake now, in Milan, after a restful week on the lakes. Milan is a pleasant reality to me no matter how ugly it gets.

The fog over the lake still lingered this morning. It was to be the last fog before Spring would make its complete and grand entrance in the northern part of the country. Just as I am about to exit.

March 23rd   Milan

The taxis were on strike today, but I managed to find a ride out to Nuovo Macello for a nice lunch. My last in Italy.

The driver told me about how he loves New York but heard that it had changed a lot in the last ten years since he had been there. I agreed with him and after a while I asked him if Milan had also changed a lot in the last ten years. He said, "not much changes in Milan. Not much has changed in Italia."

March 24th   Zürich

It was a beautiful ride especially just over the border passing by Lugano. I regret not getting off to stay for a night. I was almost completely discombobulated by the sounds of German and my mouth would not stop saying the few Italian words and phrases I have come to be familiar with. I stupidly thought I could try some French and the reactions from people were even more dismissive. But eventually I found my way.